Serving Those Called to Serve

Serving Those Called to Serve

Reflections and Insights into the Mission, Theory, and Practice of Theological Education

Greg Henson
&
Thomas E. Phillips
editors

DTL Monographs

©Digital Theological Library 2025
Library of Congress Cataloging-in-Publication Data

Greg Henson & Thomas E. Phillips (editors).
Serving Those Called to Serve: Reflections and Insights into the Mission, Theory, and Practice of Theological Education / Greg Henson & Thomas E. Phillips, editors

197 + xv pp. cm. cm. 12.7 x 20.32 (includes bibliography)
ISBN 979-8-89731-179-8 (Print)
ISBN 979-8-89731-183-5 (Ebook)
ISBN 979-8-89731-182-8 (Kindle)
ISBN 979-8-89731-210-8 (Abridged Audio Discussion)

   1   Theological seminaries — Administration 2. Religious institutions — Administration

BV4075 .H46 2025

This Open Access book is freely available in multiple languages at www.DTLPress.com.

Cover Image: Window in Wesley Chapel, London Cover design: DTL Staff

Contents

Series Preface
ix

Editors' Preface
xiii

Part I
The Changing Context of Theological Education

Seminary Disrupted
Pak-Wah Lai
3

Wherever Theological Education Ends
B. Yuki Schwartz
13

Collaboration
Brent C. Sleasman
21

Educating to Build Just and Sustainable Communities
Gabriella Lettini
29

Metamodernism and Theological Education
Robert J. Duncan, Jr.
37

Part II
Honoring Wisdom, Experiences and Traditions from the Past

Foundations
Mark Patterson
49

The Ministry of Listening
Juliet Mousseau
61

Is (Theological) Education a Waste of Time?
Enoh Šeba
65

Reflections on the Banalization of Knowledge
Suheil Laher
73

The Wisdom of the Ages and of Age
Ora Horn Prouser
79

Part III
Innovations in Theological Education and Formation

Ready, Fire, Aim
Thomas E. Phillips
87

Practicing Innovation
Shanda Stricherz & Greg Henson
99

Widening Access in Higher Education, Opportunities and
Challenges for Students with Complex Needs
Ian Birch
111

Trinity Leadership Fellows
Robert Garris
123

Trustworthy Assessment and Pastoral Formation
Marjolein de Blois & Greg Henson
129

Part IV
On Libraries and Their Role in Theological Education

Today's Library
Kristin Johnston Largen
149

We Must Preserve Books at All Costs
Stanley E. Porter
155

Embracing Open Access Publishing in Biblical,
Theological, and Religious Studies
Drew Baker
159

On the Timeliness and Sensibleness of a Digital and
Collaborative Library
Kyle Roberts
167

The Great Benefit of the Digital Theological Library to the
Entirely Online Theological Institution
Randall J. Pannell
173

Connecting Institutional Transformation and
Decision-Making
Charisse L. Gillett
170

Empowering Global Seminaries
Thomas E. Phillips
185

Afterword
Greg Henson & Thomas E. Phillips
193

Bibliography
195

Series Preface

This series, *DTL Monographs*, shares some common features with our other series. The books in this series, like all books published by DTL Press, are Open Access, meaning that the pdfs are freely available to end users with no fees from our website (www.DTLPress.com). The books in this series, also like all books published by DTL Press, are available in print through Amazon.com (and our website). And the books in this series, again like all books published by DTL Press, are composed by scholars for an informed academic audience.

Although all DTL Press books share these three characteristics (Open Access, available in print and academically sound), the Press's series differ in other significant ways. This series, *DTL Monographs*, is distinguished from our *Theological Essentials* series, because the volumes in this series are traditionally authored, meaning that the authors penned the work using traditional authorship approaches rather than using AI to generate the work. This series, *DTL Monographs*, is distinguished from our *Open Resources for Global Theological Education*, because the volumes in this series are original publications rather than Open Access translations of well known, previously published, scholarly works.

This Series

Rigor: The primary criterion for reviewing manuscripts to be published in this series is academic quality. The Press publishes scholarly monographs (including revised dissertations) and multi-authored edited books which focus upon topics of importance to our seminary level readership. Books in this series are vetted by scholars with expertise in the field(s) addressed in the work.

Originality: Books in the series have not been previously published (in any language) and they are not derivative works created by AI. Books in this series make original contributions to scholarly discourse. The books in this series do not merely summarize or introduce scholarly discourse; they advance scholarship.

Affordability: The DTL Press is committed to the idea that affordability should not be a barrier to knowledge. *All persons are equally deserving of the right to know and to understand.* Therefore, ebook versions of all DTL Press books are available from the DTL libraries without charge, and available as print books for a nominal fee.

Accessibility: The DTL Press would like to make high quality, original scholarly monographs available to everyone, everywhere in the world. Therefore, the books in this series are made available in multiple languages to the degree warranted by the global appeal of the work. Translations are generated by AI.

An Invitation

Finally, the DTL Press is non-confessional and will publish works in any area of religious studies. We invite authors with an idea or manuscript for a traditionally authored book to contact us about publishing in this series. Both multi-authored, edited volumes (including *Festschrifts*) and single author monographs are welcome. If you share the DTL Press's commitment to rigor, originality, affordability and accessibility, contact us about changing the world of theological publishing by contributing to this series.

With high expectations,
Thomas E. Phillips
DTL Press Executive Director
www.thedtl.org
www.DTLpress.com

Editors' Preface

Greg Henson
Thomas E. Phillips

It is our pleasure to present this brief edited volume to the theological community for the edification of those who serve those who are called to serve. The essays in this volume are wide ranging, from reflections on the enduring value of a theological education, to an *encomium* for the writing and reading of books, to a discussion of the physical and social location of theological education, to a warning against banality ... and much more.

The authors who wrote for this volume are all either employees of the Digital Theological Library or administrators at seminaries with membership in the Digital Theological Libraries. The only other characteristic which the contributors share in common is that they responded with a willingness to write a personal reflection when given only the title and subtitle of the book and this brief prompt: "This book aims to share the collective wisdom of DTL community leaders for the benefit of theological educators and students alike." Thus, to be clear, the essays have been only lightly edited and they reflect the perspecitves of practitioners who are engaged daily in the formation of leaders for their faith traditions and the world. The volume is not designed to present a single perspective or to defend one cohesive thesis.

After receiving the essays, the editors collected the essays into four sections. The first part, "The Changing

Context of Theological Education," contains five sets of reflections about the contemporary context of theological education, both in the US and abroad. The second part, "Honoring Wisdom, Experiences and Traditions from the Past," contains five essays on the importance of theological education drawing upon the rich heritage left to it by those who have shaped and formed the communities of faith which we have inherited. The third part, "Innovations in Theological Education and Formation," presents essays which envisage new approaches to serving the educational and formational needs of religious students and leaders. The fourth and final part, "On Libraries and their Role in Theological Education," offers seven essays about the evolving role of theological libraries in communities of faith and their educational institutions.

When the editors conceived of this project, they offered contributors only the tentative title and the single sentence prompt provided above. No themes or directions were prescribed, and the essays were not submitted for approval or shaped to fit an editorial agenda. Contributors were invited to write from their own perspectives and experiences, which means the subjects explored in these pages reflect the genuine concerns and insights of the authors themselves.

One brief procedural note is worthy of mention. In keeping with DTL policies, we typically replaced the original urls in footnotes with permalinks from the Internet Archive. The rationale for these edits was strictly pragmatic. Permalinks from Archive.org are permanent and eliminate the risk of link rot over time. Thus, when links seem to have two urls combined into one (with two http: prefixes), they are a single link which directs the reader to the stable permalink at the Archive. The content preserved by the

Archive is identical to the original page on the date when the author accessed it.

With this preface in mind, we offer this volume to the theological community. May it be used well by those who continue to serve those who are called to serve. May the readers of this volume be challenged and equipped to better serve their students, colleagues, and communities of faith.

Greg Henson
Thomas E. Phillips

Part I

The Changing Context of Theological Education

Theological education does not exist in a vacuum. It is carried out in the midst of cultural shifts, technological developments, and institutional transitions that are reshaping the wider world. The essays in this section take up those realities directly, describing how the context of ministry and learning has changed and continues to change. By bringing those changes into focus, the reflections prepare us to consider how theological education can remain faithful while adapting to new conditions.

Seminary Disrupted
Reflections on Future of Theological Education

Pak-Wah Lai

The last decade has seen a persistent enrollment decline for many US and UK seminaries. Some of the largest evangelical schools, like Trinity Evangelical Divinity School (TEDS) and Gordon Conwell, have experienced a 44-50% dip while up to 50% of the 53 Bible colleges in UK are expected to close by 2030.[1] Although there are no official figures, anecdotal evidence suggests a similar though not so drastic picture among seminaries in Singapore (where the author works). Among the many reasons for this decline, one key reason is well described by Graham Tomlin, President of St Mellitus College: "Christians today were less interested in giving up their jobs to go and live at a college for a three-year residential course, especially with much less certainty of a job in your denomination at the end of it."[2]

---

[1] TED announced recently in April 2025 that it has been acquired by Trinity Western University in Canada. "The Census Enrollment Trends," *In Trust Centre for Theological Schools* (accessed 24 March 2025): https://web.archive.org/web/20250000000000*/https://www.intrust.org/in-trust-magazine/issues/winter-2024/the-census-enrollment-trends; "Trinity Western University and Trinity Evangelical Divinity School expand impact of global Christian education," *Trinity Western University* (accessed 10 April 2025): https://web.archive.org/web/20250000000000*/https://www.twu.ca/news-events/news/trinity-western-university-and-trinity-evangelical-divinity-school-expand-impact.

[2] "Are Half of UK Bible Colleges about to Close?" *News Analysis Premier Christianity* (accessed 24 March 2025): https://web.archive.org

This essay will reflect on how seminaries got to where we are, that is, a state of disruption, and explore ways we can navigate these challenges. We begin by considering the evolution of seminaries over the last 500 years and the challenges that they now face in the 21st century. We then conclude by exploring how one Singaporean seminary, BGST (where the author works), is addressing these concerns in its context.

Seminary Evolved: A History Survey

The modern concept of seminaries, as we know it, was invented in the mid 16th century, when the Council of Trent decreed "the founding of 'seminaries' for the training of clergy." The model it adopted was that of Christian monasteries, where (typically young and single, celibate) males were cloistered in resident "communities of study and character formation." In due course, this model was taken on board first by Protestants in the US and UK, and, subsequently, by many seminaries worldwide, with little change to the demographics, until the last 2-3 decades.[1]

The 17th century saw the rise of modern science whose "critical objectivity" and epistemic certainty was soon regarded as a benchmark for all academic studies, including the humanities. Theological education came under this influence from the 19th century onwards, with seminaries putting more emphasis on cognitive learning.[2] This became more pronounced from the early 1930s when accreditation bodies, like the Association of Theological

---

/web/20250000000000*/https://www.premierchristianity.com/news-analysis/are-half-of-uk-bible-colleges-about-to-close/18058.article.

[1] Justo L Gonzalez, *The History of Theological Education* (Nashville, TN: Abingdon, 2015), 221.

[2] Gonzalez, 222.

Schools (ATS), began to compel their members to offer training at the postbaccalaureate level.[1] Such professionalising of theological education, notes Linda Cannell, divorced seminary training from the theological praxis of the Church and Christian communities, and led often to a failure in the character and spiritual formation of seminarians.[2] As a result, many laity began to doubt the value of theological education and even thought of "biblical and theological studies as a matter for specialists," and no longer an "expression of loving God with all our minds."[3] As Steve Garber warns,

> for most of the globe the theological task has been short-circuited. We in the West have exported the distortion of a bifurcated, compartmentalized theology and many if not most Asian theologians teaching in seminaries have been theologically circumcised in the West.[4]

21st Century Contexts: Seminary Disrupted

The 21st century ushered in yet more disruptions for seminaries. Firstly, economic and demographic shifts. The cost of theological education has escalated significantly over the last 3 decades, while salaries for pastors and other Christian ministry professionals have remained depressed. The rapid inflation growth, compounded with the fact that

---

[1] In Asia, many seminaries still offer bachelors in theology, but the cognitive bias remains the same.

[2] Linda M. Cannell, "Theology, Spiritual Formation and Theological Education: Reflections Toward Application," *Life in the Spirit: Spiritual Formation in Theological Perspective* (ed. George Kalantzis and Jeffrey P Greenman; Downers Grove, IL: InterVarsity Press, 2010), 230-35; Linda Cannell, *Theological Education Matters: Leadership Education for the Church* (Newburgh, IN: EDCOT Press, 2006).

[3] Gonzalez, *The History of Theological Education*, 221.

[4] Steve Garber, "Interdisciplinary Study," 27 January 2023. (Unpublished email).

many seminarians are now married men and women seeking to feed their families, mean that much fewer can afford full time residential studies.

Secondly, technological changes. With the advent of Web 2.0, the traditional cognitive theological contents that were available previously only in brick-and-mortar seminaries are now offered from a whole host of digital platforms from YouTube and Spotify Podcasts to educational platforms like the Bible Project, SeminaryNow, and Coursera. Often, these are provided either for free or at a much lower cost.

Thirdly, the perceived irrelevance of seminary education. Seminary graduates are often over-trained in cognitive theological content which have limited applications in Christian discipleship and ministry. On the other hand, they are frequently undertrained in people management and ministry skills which easily takes up 80% of their work. Furthermore, theological education is often Western or US centric, and pre-occupied with Western concerns. As a Filipino theologian once remarked to me, many Western trained theological educators are often caught up in the debates between predestinarian Calvinists and Arminians, while very few have reflected theologically about the abject poverty and sufferings that many are experiencing in the majority world.

In disruption innovation theory, an industry underserving its customers is usually ripe for disruption.[1] This is certainly the case for seminaries. The high financial costs of seminary education, perceived irrelevance of

---

[1] Tony Ulwick, "When Is a Market Ripe for Disruption?" *Strategyn* (27 February 2012): https://strategyn.com/when-is-a-market-ripe-for-disruption/. For more details on disruptive innovation, see Joshua Gans, *The Disruption Dilemma* (Cambridge: MIT Press, 2017), 36.

seminary training, and the fact that theological contents are now easily offered through affordable digital platforms, mean that seminary education is now being disrupted and replaced by right sized digital theological contents available anytime, anywhere at a fraction of the cost, and often with greater relevance.

In face of such drastic challenges, it is not easy for seminaries to reinvent themselves. Firstly, the system architecture of most brick-and-mortar seminaries mean that they still have to spend millions maintaining their physical buildings and assets which, unfortunately, now serve fewer and fewer students.[1] Secondly, strategic decisions in schools are often dominated by one key stakeholder: the theological faculty. Others like the students, churches and potential employees are less involved in the strategic conversations. Unless they are unicorns, most faculty are specialists, not strategists familiar with how to align a school's strategy and products with the needs of the 'market' (e.g., students, churches, or Christian organisations). Furthermore, theologians, like most industry specialists, often privilege theological learning and educational programmes which are interesting and important to themselves but have little relevance to the needs of churches and ordinary Christians. As I look back to my 15 years as a theological educator, this is often the mistake I make. My theological bias is to teach more cognitive and technical contents in church history, and to think less about the spiritual and ministry skills formation of our students.

Thirdly, in crises like this, courageous, wise and experienced leadership is called for. Yet, it is often difficult to recruit such a Principal/ President. The candidate must not only have advanced theological training (i.e., a PhD),

---

[1] Gans, *The Disruption Dilemma*, 55.

but is also competent in strategizing, marketing, operations management, fundraising and people management, a unicorn, in other words. As a fellow Principal remarks, the faculty team is simply not the natural pipeline for developing the next generation's President. Together, these factors make it immensely harder for seminaries to redefine and align themselves to better serve their stakeholders.

Reinventing Theological Education

All seminaries operate in different theological, geopolitical, cultural and organisational contexts. Their particular callings also differ. Consequently, their strategic priorities and approaches must adapt accordingly. This is certainly the case for BGST, which I now offer as an illustration of how one seminary in Singapore is trying to reinvent the way it provides theological education while remaining faithful to its original vision.

Founded in 1989 by two Bible-Presbyterian (B-P) churches, BGST is now known as an evangelical school where Anglicans, Methodists, Presbyterians, Brethren, Lutherans, B-Ps and others learn with and from one another. Where we differ from other local seminaries is that the school's mission is not to train pastors and missionaries (even though they are most welcome) but to provide postgraduate theological education for marketplace Christians, so that they can be "theologically mature as they are professionally competent" wherever God calls them.[1] To this day, most of our students work in the civil service, schools, technological sectors, finance industries and so on. Many fewer are in professional Christian ministries,

---

[1] I thank Steve Garber for this succinct summary of why we train marketplace Christians.

engaging in pastoring or missions work. What they all share in common, however, is that they are all part time students (i.e., studying in evening and weekend classes), and require a flexible learning environment that caters to their manifold work, ministry and family commitments.

While much can be said as to how the school navigates its legacy and contexts, I will focus on just one area: how is BGST reframing and redesigning its theological programmes and courses so that its primary audience, marketplace Christians, can be equipped to be more effective ambassadors for Christ (2 Cor 5:20) in the Church and their diverse marketplaces. That Christians may mediate the love, truth, and holiness of Christ wherever they work and serve?

Firstly, we recognize that we are not the local churches and thus cannot provide the natural environment for continual discipleship. Yet, as a parachurch, we can support churches with specialised educational services so that they can better disciple their marketplace Christians. My analogy for this is the relationship between family doctors and medical specialists. Family doctors cater to the general and daily medical needs of most people but sometimes require the help of medical specialists and surgeons to address specific medical ailments.

Secondly, we seek to be faithful to our legacy and vision: BGST is called to serve the marketplace Christians. To be effective, however, we must accept the fact that most marketplace Christians will never require postgraduate education to fulfil their calling. Consequently, we are embarking on a journey of right sizing and designing our training from developing shorter workshops and practicums to creating short digital learning modules for church small groups, so that we can reach and equip more marketplace Christians.

Thirdly, undergirding the above is a recognition that marketplace Christians not only need theological formation but also spiritual and ministry skills formation, what is popularly known as training the "Head, Heart and Hands." Christians must not only know our Triune God intellectually but also grow in His love experientially and serve His people effectively. This calls for substantial spiritual formation and ministry skills training so that students are better prepared to serve and lead which typically take up to 80% of their work and ministry. Such practical training, however, often do not meet the standards of accreditation bodies. One accreditation system that the author is familiar with, for example, allows for only 10% of a theological programme to be made up of practicum credits. Nevertheless, to deliver more impactful training, we accept the fact that we must operate within such accreditation constraints and will offer courses that are not accredited.

Fourthly, to be an effective ambassador for Christ, marketplace Christians must lead well both personally and as thought leaders. The former is grounded in their personal spiritual and self-leadership. To address this, BGST has begun to offer spiritual direction and formation services to deepen our students' prayer life and love for Christ. The latter requires a theological learning environment where students can reflect constantly on how to contextualise their faith at work and in their industries. To this end, we are in the process of reframing our postgraduate courses so that students can reflect critical on the marketplace implications of their theological learning. Shorter micro-credential workshops are also being designed for the same purposes.

Conclusion

The 21st century is the worst and best of times for seminaries. It is worst because we are discovering that the way we deliver theological education is now being challenged and regarded increasingly as irrelevant. Indeed, not a few schools' existence is now in question. It is, however, also the best of times because the crisis is forcing us rethink what does it mean to provide effective and impactful theological education? Rather than resigning ourselves to the disruption, we can take this as an opportunity to transform ourselves so that we can better equip Christians to participate in God's purposes for them (Eph 2:10). What I have suggested above for BGST is structured and designed according to the school's particular contexts; we are small and limited in resources, evangelical/non-denominational, and serves a particular clientele: marketplace Christians. How the transformation plays out for other seminaries, however, will look very different depending on their specific contexts. It is my prayer that BGST's story may provide some food for thought for how others can adapt and transform to better serve God's kingdom!

Dr Lai Pak Wah is Principal and Lecturer in Church History and Marketplace Theology at the Biblical Graduate School of Theology (BGST). Dr Lai has taught and researched in a wide range of subjects, including early church history, science and faith, Chinese medicine, digital disruptions, marketplace ethics, and leadership. He is also the author of *The Dao of Healing: Christian Perspectives on Chinese Medicine* and a certified Belbin coach. He and his family worships at Mt Carmel Bible Presbyterian Church where he is the Elder overseeing Evangelism and Leadership Development.

The vision of **Biblical Graduate School of Theology** is to equip every Christian to be an ambassador for Christ in the Church and their marketplaces. The school provides a wide range of learning for marketplace students from postgraduate studies, spiritual formation, leadership formation and discipleship training.

Wherever Theological Education Ends
"Where are you located now?"

B. Yuki Schwartz

Whenever I do any kind of public engagements representing Claremont School of Theology (CST) as a member of the dean's office, the same question comes up: *"Where are you located now?"*

It's a logical question, considering the many moves that the school has made. In the past 10 years, CST has moved from Claremont, CA, to Oregon, then back to Claremont, and finally to our current home in west Los Angeles. CST also has created international programs and counts students from dozens of different countries among our student population, which adds additional layers to our peripatetic past and present.

CST has not been the only theological school in the US that has grappled with the downsizing, moving campus, or loss of institutional property. In her book *Attempt Great Things for God*, Chloe T. Sun names CST among other mainline seminaries that have left large campuses to merge with other institutions such as colleges or large churches or have closed outright. Such moves are "signs of the times that include declining enrollment and ongoing financial difficulties" that many US theological learning institutions are facing.[1] Alumni, faculty, supporters, and prospective

---

[1] Chloe T. Sun, *Attempt Great Things for God: Theological Education in Diaspora* (Theological Education Between the Times; Grand Rapids: William B. Eerdmans Publishing Company, 2020), 41.

students across theological education are raising questions or concerns about what a school's move from a large campus with dozens of buildings to a few rooms totaling a few thousand square feet means for their futures. Like their biblical ancestors, they wonder how to sing the songs from religious and spiritual traditions by the banks of rivers that are not their denominational or community's ancestral lands.

This is a matter of affect as well as a pragmatic one. Where theological education happens matters to students, faculty, staff, and alumni as much as what theological education teaches. Our vocational becomings, or our opening up to the endless potentialities and possibilities of their vocations as academic scholars, religious professionals, and spirituality-informed leaders, literally takes place in classrooms whose windows open to vistas of city blocks or lush lawns, among library stacks, and in cozy campus dorm rooms or student apartments. We ache when we leave those spaces and grieve when they are lost. We wonder: How do we create the intimacies that theological education is known for when we don't have the space to do it?

There's no getting around it: Theological education is at its end, in time and in space. But what theological education is learning is that it is at the end where the intimacies of becoming flourish most powerfully, "where the flowing potentiality of each actuality, each creature, realizes itself in limitation."[1] More than the end of a history of Western dominance in theological education, the loss of property invites serious reflection and the creation of new practices for doing theological education wherever it

---

[1] Catherine Keller, *Face of the Deep: A Theology of Becoming* (New York and London: Routledge, 2003), 7.

happens, because this *topos* has defined both religious and settler-colonial identities and their meanings of success for generations.

Let's be honest: This unhomedness, this wandering, this lostness in unacknowledged and contested territories that educators and learners now find ourselves in isn't new. Theological scholars have been researching and still research what their spiritual traditions have to say about diasporas, migrations, border experiences, displacements, exiles, genocides, and colonizations. More and more students are entering their theological studies with intimate experiences of the violence, hunger, terror, and assaults that occur under loss of land, which includes military and political conquests, economic neocolonization, and the economic exiles of homelessness. A multimillion-dollar institution's loss of its own property does not compare to what they have been or are living through. But it does invite those of us in the offices that create the structures of support for students, faculty, and staff to reimagine how to learn and thrive when no place is permanent and everything is possible. The end of theological education can also be a goal to learn in places where we have not gone before.

That is, we have an opportunity to try and learn choratically.

To learn choratically, or to learn from the chora, the depths of the empty or inchoate spaces that exist outside of the traditional or mainstream structures of ordering, means to acknowledge and live out of the in-betweenness of the moment that we are intimately moving within. In his powerful book *Eschatology and Space*, Vitor Westhelle connects the chora to the kairos of Christian political theologies. Where kairos speaks of the unfolding depths of time that overflow or seep beyond the clock or calendar, the chora is the flowering and multitudinous spaces that cannot remain contained within the boundaries and borders of geography. The chora is not the utopia of the heavens or the eutopia of fantasy (or even the dystopia of science fiction). The chora is the eschatological space that exists not-yet-here and not-quite there. Westhelle writes:

> Choratic spaces are spaces of transition and therefore of trial. They are margins in which possibilities can be born but where the tragic, the terrible lurks, and annihilation impends. This explains why in these spaces hope and despair are so closely associated and why they are religious spaces par excellence, where fascination and terror meet—as in the apt description of the holy by Rudolf Otto: *fascinans et tremendum*.[1]

I can't think of a better description for theological learning at the moment, when fewer students and faculty are able to move to the places where their theological schools are based. Students are already learning choratically as they attempt to balance their studies against work, family, pastoral, and community responsibilities, all of which take place in their own respective realms. Student demand for online courses over in-person courses is born out of such choratic needs. Choratic learning together acknowledges the dangers and instabilities we are each facing to ask what is necessary so that all members of the learning community can co-teach and co-learn in this unformed space together, by whatever tactics we create. The past ways of learning, such as in-person classes or residential programs, are not lost but occur alongside the lamentation for the past, the experiments of the now, and the hope-filled imaginings of whatever is to come, wherever it comes. Similar to the feminist diasporic imagination that Kwok Pui-lan describes, which negotiates "an ambivalent

---

[1] Vitor Westhelle, *Eschatology and Space: The Lost Dimension in Theology Past and Present* (New York: Palgrave Macmillan, 2012), 100-01.

past, while holding on to fragments, memories, cultures, and histories in order to dream of a different future,"[1] choratic learning imagines and practices education through contradictory and multiple ways, bringing intersectional perspectives and voices to give shape to our possibilities. Choratic theological education emerges through the loss or transition of spaces and certainties and dwells and works in solidarity with students and the communities that surround them.

Because choratic learning happens in-process, or while in the daily practices of different community members finding one another to teach and learn together, intentionality is vital. Intentionality is the concerted effort of making visible that which was assumed (such as study habits, tech literacy, and Euroamerican notions about time management), in favor of recovering invisibilized ways of knowing and learning and experimenting with what works for different bodies and neurotypes. The community that once came about because of proximity becomes through effort and deliberation. Opportunities and spaces are crafted for the purpose of helping learners hold on to one another and buoy each other up, instead of leaving one another to drown. That's part of the memory-keeping of the chora, re-membering the victims of the march of historical progress that valorized growth as insurance against an uncertain future, and letting the wounded and lost guide us in imagining the world other-wise.

Westhelle notes that theology rarely confronts the reality of eschatology, or the real-world genocides, border conflicts, wards, and suffering that much of the world

---

[1] Kwok Pui-lan, *Postcolonial Imagination and Feminist Theology* (Louisville: Westminster John Knox Press, 2005), 48.

experiences, including many members of theological learning communities.

> Winners don't want to "talk eschatological" about a subject that their victims alone have a claim upon, a claim that will haunt every generation until justice is done. And this justice, this making right, this justification, can only be the lot of those who have undergone the eschatological crossing.[1]

It is fitting, then, that theological learning spaces now find ourselves in the same chora as our subjects and students. Our liberation is clearly bound up with theirs; we cannot be made right until we help make the worlds that they live in right, too.

There's a small cottage industry right now in theological education that's geared toward helping us imagine or invent the future, still based on the metrics of the past rooted in numerical growth and institutional influence. There are lots of experiments happening and I'm thrilled about that! But as I read about different options and strategies for the future, I keep in mind Westhelle's description of tactics for navigating the eschaton, as opposed to the strategies of empires. Drawing on the work of Michel de Certeau, Westhelle wrote that tactics are the ways in which we struggle through the end, found in the practices and works of everyday life and the genuine intimacies that spring forth from them. None of this can be invented but can only happen in the doing. The next movement for theological education may be in meeting students in the places where they are and lingering there with them to see what gets generated with them.

This doesn't mean leaving what we had behind. Pictures of our former campus still hang in our new space,

---

[1] Westhelle, *Eschatology and Space*, 139.

and we frequently remember the intimate moments that we created as a community even as we traverse new ones in-between together. These photos and stories invite us to ask; What do we want to re-member from that space? What was the cost of being there? How was that our space when it existed on stolen indigenous lands, anyway? How do we take the subjects we study about the loss of *topos* and turn it toward pedagogies and epistemes of chora? How do we resist the calls to just create another instance of empire and instead honor the courage of our fellow co-learners and co-teachers to learn choratically?

I don't have answers for this, since they are still being created in the unfinished and still-in-process community spaces that make up theological education today. Westhelle ends his book with a clue to where we might look together for the next steps. He paints an image of standing in the middle of a busy public space and urges his readers to stay in the chaos and look at the people who cannot leave it, the unsheltered and the lost. He writes:

> They alone ... are the ones who will point you gracefully to the exit or invite you to stay along. And, just know that you may lose the ability of knowing what is an entrance and an exit, what is beautiful and what is deplorable, since both are equidistant from the same beginning and the same end.[1]

Students in theological education are already in the chora. By meeting them there and re-imagining ourselves in ways to serve them where we meet them, there is a hope for theological education in the wherever that we find our ends.

---

[1] Westhelle, *Eschatology and Space*, 140.

B. Yuki Schwartz is an associate professor of constructive theologies and spiritualities, and associate dean of academics and assessment at Claremont School of Theology.

Claremont School of Theology (CST) is a private graduate theological institution in California, founded in 1885 (originally as the Maclay School of Theology) and historically affiliated with the United Methodist Church. Situated in Los Angeles today after relocating from its original Claremont campus, CST positions itself at the intersection of academic rigor, faithful practice, and social transformation. While rooted in a Methodist heritage, it embraces ecumenical and interreligious engagement, shaping leaders who pursue justice, belonging, and compassion across diverse traditions. Its programs include master's, doctoral, and ministry degrees, and its curriculum emphasizes contextual theologies, interreligious dialogue, and praxis in public life.

Collaboration
One Kingdom, One King, One Kingdom Mission

Brent C. Sleasman

Accepting the call to serve as President of Winebrenner Theological Seminary required several major transitions: leaving a tenured faculty position for an executive leadership role, relocating from Pennsylvania to Ohio, and shifting from undergraduate education to the graduate level. I also moved from a focus on a single discipline, human communication, to engagement with the broader field of theological education.

This transition involved both tangible and intangible changes. Tangible factors included the responsibilities of the role, its place within the organizational structure, and geographic relocation. One important intangible was the posture toward peer schools. In an industry often shaped by anxiety over the "demographic cliff," other schools were too often viewed as competitors, and student recruitment became a zero-sum game. In contrast, this essay presents a different vision, one that required a significant level of "un-learning" and relearning and represents one of the most significant insights that I wish to pass on to others in the field of theological education. This vision is one that prioritizes collaboration and partnership over competition.

Before diving deeper, it's important to name a few assumptions that frame my reflections. These are not meant as universal prescriptions but as context for Winebrenner's organizational shift and my own leadership journey. First, at Winebrenner, we interpret "theological" in the Digital Theological Library as reflecting a Christ-centered perspective. Discipleship is our core task. Second, we affirm the Old and New Testaments as foundational for guiding our mission. These two assumptions shape how we understand and pursue our work.

One Kingdom, One King, One Kingdom Mission

A Jesus-centered, biblically grounded approach to organizational leadership leads to conclusions that differ significantly from what I encountered as an undergraduate faculty member. Rather than forcing students into a narrow set of options, we can expand possibilities by integrating theological convictions into our leadership. Scripture reshapes our organizational practices, moving us from a mindset of competition to one of collaboration, and from rivalry to shared purpose. While we still operate in a competitive landscape, theological education benefits far more from shared wisdom and mutual support than from organizational rivalry. What follows explores each element of the guiding phrase: *One Kingdom, One King, One Kingdom Mission.*

One Kingdom

Accepting the Genesis creation account as true leads us to recognize that from the beginning, there has only been one kingdom, God's. Yet, the biblical narrative reveals Israel's growing desire to imitate surrounding nations, culminating in their demand for a human king. God's words to Samuel in 1 Samuel 8:7 are striking: "It is not you they have rejected, but they have rejected me as their king." Every strategic planning session or governance retreat should begin with the reminder that we are participants in God's already-established kingdom.

This awareness requires humility. We are not the architects of our own kingdoms, we are born into God's. A simple, reflective question helps keep this perspective grounded: *Do I truly believe God's kingdom takes precedence over my own ambitions, or over Winebrenner's?*

This humility deepens when we acknowledge that God's mission continues, with or without us. Esther 4:14 is often quoted: "Who knows but that you have come to your royal position for such a time as this?" But we too easily overlook the earlier part of the verse: "If you remain silent at this time, relief and deliverance for the Jews will arise from another place..." In short, God's purposes are not dependent on our survival or success. His kingdom endures, even if our organizations do not.

One King

To fulfill His divine purpose, God appointed His Son, Jesus, as King of His singular kingdom. Revelation 17:14 and 19:16 affirm that Jesus is the "King of kings." His centrality in Kingdom work cannot be overstated. This is why the Association of Theological Schools (ATS) emphasizes spiritual and biblical formation and why the study of both Old and New Testaments remains essential for theological educators and students. The Old Testament sets the stage; the New Testament reveals Jesus fulfilling God's Kingdom mission.

Of course, not all who serve in theological education place Jesus at the center. What I offer here is one particular perspective, rooted in a Christ-centered vision.

This perspective also requires humility. While I may "lead" a seminary, I do so under the ultimate leadership of Jesus. Leadership can be isolating, but remembering that Jesus is King invites me into ongoing conversation with Him about challenges, responsibilities, and the care of those

I lead. It also pushes against cultural values that idolize leaders. When we say: "there is a King, and I am not Him," we take a bold step away from self-centeredness and toward a Christ-centered orientation.

One Kingdom Mission

Recognizing the pre-existence of God's Kingdom and Jesus' authority as King raises an essential question: *How can we participate in God's ongoing Kingdom work?*

This question contrasts sharply with common Boardroom inquiries such as "What is our mission?" or "What is our strategic plan?" Instead of inventing a mission, we are called to steward the one God has already begun. That means acknowledging God's Kingdom predates our organizations and affirming that Jesus, not a president or Board, is the true leader of the seminary.

This mindset even reorients the hiring process. Rather than prioritizing candidates with narrowly defined "professional identities" and best practices imported from other sectors, we seek individuals who recognize God's mission already at work and are eager to explore its unique expression in our context.

It also leads to another question: Can a mission ever be "fulfilled"? Can a seminary's mission be "completed"? From a Kingdom perspective, the answer is "yes." A school may close while God's mission continues. While such closures involve loss, we must not confuse human grief with the larger unfolding of God's work.

Each school has its own story, yet ATS data show that most students apply to only one institution, indicating that our primary challenge is not competition from peer schools but disengagement from theological education itself. My own thinking continues to shift away from pursuing a "unique mission" toward embracing God's already unfolding mission.

And what is that mission? In a word: discipleship. (See Matthew 28 and Luke 4.)

Collaboration
Where Stewardship Meets Discipleship

People often step away from collaborative efforts because of branding concerns, financial disagreements, lack of imagination, or resistance to change. I've encountered all of these. Early in my career, the prevailing mindset was competitive: students chose one school, and that meant another school lost. This zero-sum thinking is reinforced by higher education rankings that reward exclusivity over access.

But God's Kingdom is eternal, while our methods must be flexible and responsive. One small but important shift is reconsidering what we measure. Instead of asking "Who gets to 'count' the student?" we might ask, "How many collaborative partnerships are we cultivating?" or "How many of our students are taking classes elsewhere?" These questions prompt us to rethink outdated systems and metrics in favor of Kingdom-oriented values.

Collaboration also requires us to keep costs low and build adaptable structures that welcome innovation. Too often, theological disagreements result in combative "culture wars" that divide us. We need new metaphors; we need language rooted in ecosystems and mutual flourishing, not militaristic division.

Though many speak of collaboration, few practice it deeply. Yet Scripture invites us into hospitality, shared purpose, and Kingdom partnership. When we stop viewing each other as competitors and start seeing each other as co-laborers, new possibilities open up for impact and faithfulness.

Conclusion

My journey as President of Winebrenner Theological Seminary has taught me that Scripture must shape how I lead. That means aligning my theological convictions with how I guide the institution. The principles described here apply across a wide range of settings, from churches to denominations, church camps to seminaries. Our aim should be to develop a shared "operating system" rooted in discipleship and designed for flexibility, offering multiple pathways for learners and followers of Jesus.

In *Designing the New American University*, Michael Crow and William Dabars describe "isomorphism," the tendency of institutions to imitate one another. This dynamic is also present in theological education. Internal financial pressures and external forces alike lead seminaries to adopt similar models, which ironically undermine true distinctiveness. Innovation requires courage, especially from boards and presidents.

To resist this trend, we must reclaim our distinctiveness and boldness. When we embrace our unique histories and keep Jesus at the center, we expand our creative capacity to participate in God's unfolding Kingdom mission.

Brent C. Sleasman is President of Winebrenner Theological Seminary in Findlay, Ohio. His research and writing examine aspects of philosophy of communication as expressed in various faith-based and organizational contexts. He is co-editor of *Sacred Rhetoric: Discourses in Identity and Meaning*, author of *Albert Camus' Philosophy of Communication: Making Sense in an Age of Absurdity* and editor of *Creating Albert Camus: Foundations and Explorations of His Philosophy of Communication*. Additionally, he is a contributing author to *Communication Theory and Millennial Popular Culture, The Electronic Church in the Digital Age, Phoenix Rising, The Sage Encyclopedia of Identity*, and *The Social History of American Families*. He serves on the editorial board of the *Journal of Communication and Religion*.

Winebrenner Theological Seminary was established in 1942 as a graduate school of theology of Findlay College (renamed The University of Findlay in 1989). The Theological Seminary exists to *equip leaders for service in God's kingdom*. Winebrenner was founded by the Churches of God, General Conference (CGGC), an evangelical denomination headquartered in Findlay, Ohio. The Seminary derives its name from the founder of the denomination, John Winebrenner, who established the group in 1825 in Harrisburg, Pennsylvania. Winebrenner continues to serve the CGGC as its sole seminary as well as students from diverse denominational backgrounds. In 1961, Winebrenner received its charter from the State of Ohio, to become a free-standing and independent, degree-granting organization and today sits adjacent to The University of Findlay. The current strategic priorities include an emphasis on Stewardship, Discipleship, and Collaboration.

Educating to Build Just and Sustainable Communities

Gabriella Lettini

Sometimes I think of myself as the "Accidental Dean." I never had vocational aspirations to be an academic administrator until I was asked to serve as such by Rev. Dr. Rebecca Parker, then president of Starr King School for the Ministry (SKSM) in Berkeley, CA, a Unitarian Universalist and multireligious seminary. I had arrived at SKSM to be an educator, drawn by Dr. Parker's work, who had written that the purpose of education is humanization in the context of dehumanizing forces and realities and witnessing the abiding presence of healing, sustaining, and transforming grace: "To be an educator is to cooperate with revolutionary grace in the work of sustaining and restoring soul." As I became an academic dean and later also a Chief Academic Officer, I had to reframe both my understanding of my vocation and of what an academic administrator is. I joined Starr King because of its commitment to "Educating to Counter Oppression and Build Just and Sustainable Community" (ECO-CJSC). How could I embrace this commitment in my new role, as I did in my teaching and scholarship? Academic administration did not initially strike me as the place where crucial transformative work happens, as I saw it more as necessary upkeeping. I was both right and wrong.

"We Teach by Who We Are"

At Starr King, we often stress that "we teach by who we are," quoting emerita president Rev. Rosemary Bray McNatt. My first learning in my new role was that this is also profoundly true as an administrator: students learned from the way we do administration just as much as in class and are often even more critical about the ways our professed mission matches our choices and actions. This is both motivating and terrifying. I learned to see academic leadership as another way to embody our values and the mission of the school, yet this also meant that the stakes felt even higher, and the possibilities for disappointing people and myself even more dire.

Embracing "both-and"

The late Dr. Ibrahim Abdurrahman Farajajé was another vital leader, educator, and mentor who had attracted me to Starr King and profoundly shaped all aspects of my work there. All his teaching challenged binary understandings and ideas of purity, inviting us to acknowledge the utter complexity of life and embrace a "both-and" approach. Learning to be even more comfortable with the complexities, ambiguities, and unresolved tensions in my work and life has been one of the ongoing learning experiences as an administrator, and something I constantly must remind people of. Often, people come to me with exact ideas and requests about how something should be done. In my role, I need to lift the whole complex picture of who we are as an institution and educational community, with diverse needs and opinions on the specific ways our mission and commitment to justice should be embodied.

One straightforward example is the way we organize our course offerings and class calendar. It is never simple, now that we are a distributed community with people residing all over the country and even abroad, where most students work full-time jobs and have childcare and parent care responsibilities. Often, a group of students from a specific demographic makes a request, claiming that it is the right thing to do. For instance, why don't we offer only asynchronous courses, or synchronous, or evenings, or weekend courses? Even in a multireligious community, people can make assumptions about the sacred observances we should all celebrate, and what they deem less relevant.

One simple yet vital role that I have is to remind the community about who we are, trying not to erase or silence anyone. This paradoxically also means that no one is ever fully satisfied with any decision, something that challenges basic consumer culture assumptions and notions of entitlement. Leaning into this partial frustration as a space for growth and grace has been essential learning for me, and I hope for my community. How do we consider all people's needs, centering the needs of people traditionally most oppressed and marginalized, learning to find creative solutions that also require more flexibility and adaptability from people usually entitled to a great deal of comfort? How can we advocate not only for ourselves but also for each other? Academic administration is, therefore, a place of constant testing of our values, where simple details are seldom trivial but reflect essential considerations. In other words, academic administration is a place where we can test how we understand and try to embody our theological and ethical values. One major lesson in humility is that it is hard to do.

Justice

Thomas Starr King, the Unitarian preacher and abolitionist after whom our school is named, wrote that

"There can be no such thing as justice, until human beings, in large masses, are rightly related to each other."

This quote continues to challenge me, and any narrow understanding of what is the "just thing to do" for any particular person in the school community. Justice within the school is relational and contextual, and it is connected to larger justice issues in the world. No one exists independently from the whole, and no one is righteous independently from the rest.

Academic administration, like teaching or ministering, should never be seen as individual effort, personal achievement, individual satisfaction, sanctification, or perfection. All of these activities are best seen as collective endeavors, labor in service of the community and the larger world, as we are all interrelated parts of the same organism.

Collective Labor

To remind ourselves that all ministry is labor can be pretty helpful. A labor of love, indeed, spiritually grounded work, yet challenging labor, if engaged with seriousness and passion. To educate to build just and sustainable communities is hard work, work that is never done, is never completed, never perfectly realized or modeled. It is always a work in progress, a process of continuous learning, where we challenge each other to understand our limitations and mistakes, and review what we thought we knew. Our sacred texts and the wisdom of our spiritual traditions inform us, and new scholarship teaches us better practices. Yet, we are not dealing with a paint-by-numbers picture to duplicate, but with diverse communities with histories of oppression, suffering, and persecution that challenge us to make good decisions in a constantly changing world and academic landscape.

In academic administrators, as in other ministries, it is always helpful to remind ourselves that it's never only about us or one constituency, but about the whole and the fulfillment of our mission. It's about the collective, the good of our communities living under systemic injustices, the good as defined by people and beings who have been traditionally pushed to the margins, if not erased altogether.

The fact that this is never just about the individual is good news, as it means we don't have to strive for individual perfection, or the perfection of our group or institution, as this perfection, this moral purity, this spiritual and political superiority cannot exist in the world as it is. What exists are choices, actions, mistakes, reflections, prayer, worship, and reparations. To be sure, learning from experience and trying again, and again, and again.

While we strive to embody a loving and just community in the way we teach and administer the school, we are part of a complex web marred by systemic historical injustices. As we try to transform ourselves and society, we are shaped by it. To be surprised by this realization, or to forget this, is not to be in touch with reality. Starr King is a School for the Ministry, an institute of higher education, not a utopia, a non-place. We look for liberating truths and ultimate beauty in sacred texts and spiritual traditions, also marred by patriarchy, racism, economic exploitation, homophobia, and queerphobia. We don't get to live at Starr King as if these were not realities, as if they did not affect us to our very core. What we do is refuse to believe that the status quo is the way things are and always will be, the last word on humanity and ourselves. We refuse to believe that injustice is justifiable and irreversible; we refuse to believe that some of us deserve privileges obtained by the exploitation and victimization of others.

Meeting the challenges of the moment

The state of our world and the current landscape of theological education ask us to fight for survival and sustainability. It challenges us to find solutions that meet the needs of our students and communities, as they live through ongoing multiple crises. Understandably, we live in a constant climate of urgency and search for innovative solutions. Starr King has been visionary and innovative before, starting online education in the early 2000s, and experimenting with different modalities of learning that are valued now, but were seen with suspicion earlier on. Yet having been an innovator in the past does not mean we can let go now. We always need to be tuned in to what new needs and new solutions are emerging in our communities.

One significant learning for me is that it is always wise to take the time to reground ourselves in our mission and reflect together on how a new strategy, technology, or initiative meets the mandate of our mission, and how they fall short. It is a process that must be, once again, a collaborative endeavor, so that we help each other to see things from different perspectives, realizing questions and issues we may have missed or glossed over but are essential to other constituencies. As an administrator, I hope we can continue to be deeply intentional about the decisions we make and keep transparent about them, without absolutist claims to have found the perfect solutions that everyone else should embrace.

We strive to educate to counter oppression and model what we preach as messy and limited human beings, inspired and strengthened by the same spirit that has given resilience, purpose, hope, and faith to generations and generations before us. We cooperate with forces of healing and transformation that are bigger, older, and stronger than any of us. Dr. Ibrahim Abdurrahman Farajajé reminded us that theological education, in its broadest sense, is a holistic collaboration with the divine in the healing of the universe. As he said, our spiritual transformation is both the process by which we engage in this labor and the product of our labor.

Rev. Gabriella Lettini (Ph.D.) is Aurelia Henry Reinhardt Professor of Theological Ethics, Chief Academic Officer, and Academic Dean at Starr King School for the Ministry. A native of Turin, Italy, she is also a Minister of the Waldensian Church in Italy. She has a Ph.D. in Theology from Union Theological Seminary in New York City.

Starr King School for the Ministry is a progressive Unitarian Universalist seminary in Oakland, California, with roots dating back to 1904 when it began as the Pacific Unitarian School for the Ministry. It equips students for ministry, spiritual leadership, and justice-oriented service across religious traditions, not limited to UU communities. Its educational philosophy emphasizes *Educating to Counter Oppressions*, multi-religious learning, and contextual formation in communities of faith. Among its degree offerings are the Master of Divinity (M.Div.) and Master of Arts in Social Change (M.A.S.C.), along with certificates in areas such as chaplaincy, UU studies, multi-religious studies, and psychedelic justice.

Metamodernism and Theological Education

Robert J, Duncan, Jr.

Several years ago, I read a blog from Union Theological Seminary about the future of Theological education:

> It is no secret that higher education in the U.S. increasingly faces an unprecedented set of challenges that threaten the sustainability of institutions both large and small. It also should come as no surprise to anyone paying attention that seminaries face these very same challenges and more. Without the built-in safety net of either a university or a denominational affiliation, small, independent theological schools are among the most vulnerable of all.[1]

The blog addresses sustainability as one of the most significant challenges to traditional theological education:

> To remain sustainable, theological education is going to have to meet the vocational needs of a new and more diverse constituency of students, reaching them where they are with flexible formats, creative pedagogies, and innovative credentialing opportunities that go beyond the traditional master's and doctoral degrees.[2]

---

[1] Isaac Sharp, "The Future of Theological Education at Union and Beyond," *Union Theological Seminary*, New York, June 6, 2021, (accessed 10-15-24): https://web.archive.org/web/20160101000000*/ https:// utsnyc.edu/blog/2021/06/03/the-future-of-theological-education-at-union-and-beyond/#:~:text=To%20remain%20sustainable%2C%20theological%20education,traditional%20master's%20and%20doctoral%20degrees.

[2] Sharp, (blog).

In the same blog, the president of Union responded to what the future of theological education would look like:

> "The honest answer is we don't know! No one does!" President Jones explains. "But what we do know is that the future is already emerging out of the innovative work that we are presently doing. Step by step, we are shaping the future to come, and we will adapt and shift as we go." [1]

The two most significant factors that illustrate the problem with traditional theological education are enrollment and cost. As such, there is a direct correlation between the two: enrollment is down, and the cost of attendance is up. A new approach is needed for theological education to become sustainable in the new era of metamodernity.

Metamodernism arose in the twenty-first century as an oscillation between Modernity and Postmodernity. It is characterized by creating *bubbles* from different decision-making levels and combining them to implement a previously impossible decision. Metamodernism embraces the idea that there are new ways to understand and experience life, faith, and ministry.

Metamodernism is a cultural philosophy that has emerged in response to postmodernism, seeking to move beyond its limits to reestablish hope and optimism. Metamodernism embraces paradox and juxtaposition, taking the realities of modernism and applying postmodern deconstruction, thereby creating a unique reality.

Metamodernism oscillates between the modern and the postmodern. It oscillates between a modern enthusiasm and a postmodern irony, between hope and melancholy,

---
[1] Sharp, (blog).

between naiveté and knowingness, empathy and apathy, unity and plurality, totality and fragmentation, purity and ambiguity. Indeed, by oscillating to and fro or back and forth, the metamodern negotiates between the modern and the postmodern.[1]

Metamodernism offers a novel approach to addressing postmodern skepticism, envisioning a more inclusive future where new forms of progress and knowledge can be achieved. It navigates a complex terrain by shifting between modern enthusiasm and postmodern irony.

A. Severan's book *Metamodernism and the Return of Transcendence* explores this concept of an oscillation between modernism and postmodernism.

> Ontologically, metamodernism oscillates between the modern and the postmodern. It oscillates between a modern enthusiasm and a postmodern irony, between hope and melancholy, between naivete and knowingness, empathy and apathy, unity and plurality, totality and fragmentation, purity and ambiguity. ...Each time the metamodern enthusiasm swings toward fanaticism, gravity pulls it back toward irony; the moment its irony sways toward apathy, gravity pulls it back toward enthusiasm.[2]

The oscillation present in the metamodern era incorporates postmodernism while simultaneously oscillating between what came before and what will come

---

[1] Timotheus Vermeulen and Robin van den Akker, "Notes on Metamodernism," *Journal of Aesthetics and Culture* 2.1 (2010): 56-77 (Taylor and Francis online, accessed 1/25/2025): https://web.archive.org/web/20160101000000*/https://www.tandfonline.com/doi/full/10.3402/jac.v2i0.5677.

[2] A. Severan, *Metamodernism and the Return of Transcendence* (self-pub., Metamodern Spirituality Book 1, March 25, 2021), 47, Kindle.

after. Metamodernism's oscillation provides a way of thinking that involves shifting between different perspectives, attitudes, and contexts. This oscillation can lead to a synthesis of these various perspectives, attitudes, and contexts, ultimately fostering a more nuanced understanding of the world.

My approach to a metamodern decision system utilizes an oscillated bubble that surrounds *any* decision matched with *all* of the remaining possible decisions, thereby creating an *any and all* combination encapsulated by the oscillated bubble.

Theological education plays a crucial role in furthering the understanding and potential of metamodern Christianity by providing a comprehensive understanding of its theological foundations and historical development for use in a new era. Fostering critical reflection on its contemporary relevance and engagement with current social issues is essential for maintaining relevance with those who have not reconnected with the Church after the COVID pandemic, as well as for those who have never been active in the Church.

Theological education will also need to adapt to newly developed technology and the social structures in metamodernity. The newly developed technology that holds the most promise and the most negative effect is here already: Artificial intelligence. Theological education will need to create innovative ways to adapt to the ethical use of AI in administration, curriculum, and instruction. AI is only one of the new technologies that theological education must utilize to effectively equip individuals with the practical skills to enact it within the metamodern world through new forms of community ministry, mission, and evangelism.

Adapting theological education to metamodernity will present significant challenges, including new approaches to enrollment, financial pressure, deferred maintenance, and denominational identity, which will lead to required changes. I have developed the following formula to describe the oscillation between modern and postmodern theological education:

No Bricks + All Chips = Innovation (Virtual)

Theological Schools that are embracing metamodernism are rethinking and reformulating theological education in the virtual space created by metamodern technology. Virtual theological education in the metamodern era presents a sustainable approach to theological education, utilizing a distributed faculty & staff (a staffing pattern in which an organization or school's staff is not working in a common office building but is distributed around a state, country, or the world), competency-based courses, and a ministry-focused approach. By embracing innovative technologies and strategies, virtual theological education eliminates geographical boundaries, fosters a global community of learners, and provides competency-based learning experiences for individuals seeking spiritual growth and theological understanding.

Theological education in the metamodern era explores a new instructional approach that uses an individual cohort approach and guided education. Modern and postmodern theological education employs pedagogy, which is focused on teacher-led instruction. Pedagogy is defined as:

> Pedagogy, or "leading the young," refers mainly to developing habits of thinking and acting. Within pedagogy, a teacher's main role is to provide opportunities for students to learn through experiences. For example, the coveted positions of "line leader" or "door holder" in school demonstrate the importance of

leadership and service to children. Or, when a teacher changes the volume of their voice from the playground to the classroom when speaking to students, they are exemplifying the need for behavioral awareness.[1]

Metamodern theological education employs andragogy, which is focused on student-led instruction with the teacher as a facilitator. Andragogy is defined as:

> Adults are self-driven and can rely on past experience to solve complex problems, which means that a central focus of "leading the elders" must be the question of how to best support them in retaining new ideas, learning new ways of problem solving, and strengthening independent thinking.
>
> The methods used to teach adults are different from those traditionally used to educate children. For instance, using a behavior chart with colorful stickers to motivate children to remain quiet during reading time is ineffective in adult learning. Most adult learners are already actively working in a career or field of interest, from medicine to engineering to business, and they require specialized instruction to guide and develop necessary skills. The field of adult education is constantly evolving with new practices and theories.[2]

I developed a metamodern andragogy approach at Northwind Theological Seminary by combining the oscillation between individual instruction in the modern era and cohort instruction in the postmodern era. The resulting bubble forms a previously impossible instructional approach: the Individual Cohort using Competency-based

---

[1] "Andragogy vs. Pedagogy: Key Differences in Learning," *Western Governors University* (May 24, 2022, accessed 07/14/25): https://www.wgu.edu/blog/andragogy-pedagogy-key-differences-learning2205.html.

[2] "Andragogy vs. Pedagogy," WGU

Theological Education (CBTE). The Individual Cohort (IC) approach replaces traditional courses with Outcome-based Learning Experiences (OLE), Outcome-based Experience Outlines (OLEO) replace traditional syllabi, Outcome-Based Learning Experience Assessment (OLEA) replaces traditional grading, and Individual Cohort Concentrations (ICC) replace traditional academic departments. CBTE is a specialized form of Competency-Based Education (CBE) that focuses on preparing pastors and church leaders. CBTE is based on the student demonstrating competency to complete learning experiences, which replaces students completing courses. The demonstrated competencies relate to learning experiences rooted in the student's actual ministry context.

Virtual theological education encompasses a range of online programs and courses designed to provide theological training and education through digital platforms. This approach has gained traction as institutions seek to broaden their reach and accessibility, thus enabling a more diverse student body to engage in theological studies.

One of the most notable advantages of virtual theological education is its ability to transcend geographical barriers. Students from various regions can access quality theological training that may not be available locally. Virtual learning allows students to manage their course schedule at their own pace, allowing them to balance academic obligations and personal commitments. The use of the individual cohort is one of the defining differences between postmodern and metamodern theological education. The postmodern cohort was comprised of a set of students starting and ending their degree together in a pedagogy that was instructor-led. The metamodern individual cohort comprises students progressing through their degrees, meeting together in an instructor-guided andragogy.

Virtual Faith formation is a key component of the student experience at a virtual theological institution. Traditional theological education uses face-to-face encounters with students, faculty, and advisors to develop faith formation. These encounters include chapel services, study groups, discussion groups, prayer groups, Bible study, and retreats. I have developed this description of the transition from modern faith formation to metamodern faith formation.

- Modern Faith Formation utilized groups, chapel, and 3rd-year student retreats.
- Postmodern Faith Formation used academic cohorts and mission trips.
- Metamodern Faith Formation uses a new Individual Cohort Andragogy.

At Northwind Theological Seminary, faculty mentorship is the primary connection between the student and faith formation. Northwind's "Study with Me" approach fosters interdenominational faith formation within a Big Tent of an ecumenical ministry of higher education. The metamodern era requires a rejection of the narrowing of theological views prevalent in many traditional seminaries. This narrowing of the seminary's theological view stems from assigning the lead role of the new faculty search to the existing faculty. Faculty tend to select new faculty who share or complement the dominant theological views of the current faculty. With each search, the theological view of the seminary naturally narrows. Big Tent ecumenical ministry in higher education welcomes faculty, staff, and students with various theological viewpoints while still being united in Christ.

Metamodern theological education addresses the two significant challenges of declining enrollment and increased operational costs that threaten sustainability. Adapting theological education to metamodernity is not just a choice, but a necessity. By embracing metamodernism's innovative technologies and new andragogy strategies within an oscillating metamodern bubble, virtual theological education eliminates geographical boundaries, fosters a global community of learners, and provides competency-based learning experiences for individuals seeking spiritual growth and theological understanding.

Rev. Robert J, Duncan, Jr. (DMin, ThD) is Professor of Leadershio and Specialized Ministry as well as founder and president of Northwind Consortia (Academic; Institute; Seminary; Press and Fellows). He is a retired ordained United Methodist Minister with over 40 years of ministry experience which includes pastoral ministry, pastoral counseling, planned giving, and higher education. Rob has been a frequent speaker at national conferences presenting ways to connect technology, distance education, and ministry.

Northwind Theological Seminary is an ecumenical, online seminary serving many denominations. Biblically-based with theological roots in the Wesleyan tradition, we have a strong emphasis on Contextual Ministry, Spiritual Formation, and Discipleship. Offering accessible, affordable, quality, online theological education to local pastors, bi-vocational & second career clergy, and lifelong learners for faithful and creative ministry in the NeXtChurch. The name (Northwind) points to the breath of God and the dynamic movement of the Spirit to orient the compass of our lives to true North. Symbolically, northernness is an orientation in life, a quality of character, an image and metaphor in theology and ministry, the first of the four Cardinal points of the circle to which all others are related. For C. S. Lewis and other great writers, the way to God lies to the North.

Part II

Honoring Wisdom, Experiences and Traditions from the Past

Formation for ministry has always drawn strength from the wisdom of those who came before. Practices, traditions, and stories handed down across generations continue to provide guidance for the present. The essays in this section remind us that even in a time of disruption, the past offers enduring resources that can shape and sustain faithful formation. Attention to these voices helps ensure that theological education remains rooted even as it responds to new realities.

Foundations

Mark Patterson

Introduction
The Deep Sea Diver and the Cathedral

Visitors to Winchester Cathedral, south-west of London, might be surprised to find several bronze sculptures of a deep-sea diver named William Walker. One of these is found in the garden outside the cathedral and another inside, beside which is a deep-sea diving helmet on display. While the old cathedrals of Europe commonly contain innumerable plaques, statures, and memorials, these are particularly surprising, compelling many questions. The bronze plaque only increases these:

William Walker-Diver
1869-1918
...who saved this Cathedral with his own hands
1906-1911

Who was William Walker and how could a deep-sea diver possibly save a cathedral with his own hands? The answer is both fascinating and, for our purposes reflecting upon theological education in the twenty-first century, illumining.

At the turn of the twentieth century the thousand-year-old cathedral was in grave danger of collapse. Huge cracks had appeared in the walls (some large enough for a small child to climb into) walls were bulging and leaning, and stones regularly fell from its walls. A leading architect at the time provided a dark assessment, noting that the building was sinking into the soft, wet ground and needed profound repairs if it was to be saved. A structural engineer determined that the foundation put down by the Normans nearly a thousand years earlier had been little more than a "floating raft" of birch trees, many of which had decayed and no longer existed, allowing the cathedral to slowly sink into the soft peat and clay beneath. Digging down roughly twenty feet, a bed of gravel was found and it was determined that a new foundation, set upon this footing, could be constructed to support the current structure. Because every hole dug to reach this gravel bed filled with water, this repair required a master of underwater work and thus the hiring of William Walker.

Workers dug 235 pits around (and under!) the eastern and southern ends of the cathedral, each approximately six meters deep. Walker would enter these pits, building up the foundation from the gravel beds to existing building. Walker worked six hours a day, six days a week, for six years, always in cold water and complete darkness because of the silt. Over this period, he single-handedly placed more than 25,800 bags of concrete, 114,900 concrete blocks, and 900,000 bricks. When finished, the groundwater was pumped out and the building was found to be resting solidly on its new foundation. Truly, William Walker, deep-sea diver, had saved the cathedral with his own hands. To celebrate the success, a thanksgiving service was held on 15 July 1912, at which Walker was presented a silver rose bowl by King George V, who would also later honor Walker as a member of the Royal Victorian Order (MVO).[1]

---

[1] For any who might deem such honors as insufficient, Walker also had a pub in the town of Winchester named after him. https://web.archive.org/web/20250000000000*/https://www.williamwalkerwinchester.co.uk.

While a fascinating story, it also provides a vital lesson as we turn to ponder theological education for the immediate and more distant future. *Revealed in this are two, intertwined and interrelated truths: a good foundation is vitally important if what is built upon it is to stand over time and, second, it is very difficult to repair a foundation that is insufficient or has failed.* In this tumultuous period filled with both difficulties and promise, questions and hope, this two-sided insight into our foundations is worth pondering as we consider theological education in our current setting and what "repairs" are needed to insure a long, effective, and vibrant future.

Failing Foundations: Theological Education Today

There are many reasons one might look at the state of theological education in the United States today and conclude its foundations need attention. Such an assessment is neither new nor narrowly held. Indeed, this appraisal has been voiced repeatedly for decades.

In 1994 The Murdock Charitable Trust in the Pacific northwest noticed that an increasing number of seminaries were applying for grants for financial help. This led the trust to do a study in which they interviewed roughly 800 pastors, parishioners, and seminary teachers in hope of learning why seminaries were coming under increasing financial hardship. The results were a scathing critique of American seminaries that sent a tremor through theological education across America.

In its October 24, 1994, issue, *Christianity Today* ran an article entitled "Re-engineering the Seminary? Crisis of Credibility Forces Change."[1] This article begins by

---

[1] It is worth noting that while the article raises significant criticisms it also notes new endeavors and educational models that

referencing several conclusions from the Murdock Trust report. Specifically, they list:
- Seminary students often have the same doubts as nonbelievers, see themselves as victims, and have a "deep hunger" for role models and mentoring.
- Seminaries are producing pastors the same way they did 30 years ago, are financially weakened by administrative overhead, and take little responsibility for selecting students bound for ordination.
- Lifelong tenure for professors and the accreditation process has, in some cases, been obstacles to strategic change.
- Pastors at that time were "largely satisfied" with their own job performance, but believe they were "poorly prepared" for their jobs.

Christianity Today went on to predict a coming crisis for seminaries, a strange assessment at a time when seminaries across America were seeing their greatest enrollments and highest incomes. Nevertheless, *CT* saw clouds on the horizon, noting that schools were largely out of touch with the needs of churches and the realities of parish ministry, with the needs and desires of their students who were considering or pursuing ministry, and out of touch with the times and what was needed for the church to effectively fulfill its mission within a post-Christian culture. The fact that this article was published over thirty

---

suggested positive changes were certainly occurring. The article ends with an open question: will such changes be enough? https://web.archive.org/web/20160415000000*/https://www.christianitytoday.com/ct/1994/october24/4tc074.html.

years ago should not suggest its conclusions are either solved or irrelevant; indeed, the article seems as accurate and relevant as when it first came out suggesting that such criticism remains, mutatis mutandis, largely and essentially valid and still worthy of serious consideration.

Indeed. When one looks closely across the broad swath of theological education today, we see that many of the issues noted thirty years ago remain active, characteristic, and formative.

First, the university model forming the academic paradigm of most seminaries remains largely disputational and deconstructive in method. Rather than building from faith, worship, and mission these are too often perceived as peripheral to academic interests and thus more likely to be critically appraised than taught. Moving further, across many years and many institutions, the spiritual lives of students and their own faith journeys have been largely irrelevant to the academic purpose for which institutions exist.

Second, seminaries are too often detached from the church. In the quest for academic legitimacy seminaries are "now more accountable to the academy and its guilds than to the church and its ministries, to religious studies methodology than to the theological studies and ecclesiology."[1]

Third, and growing from this, is the fact that too often the concepts taught in seminary are given little or no connection with the church and its ministries in real life settings. Students are taught about various theologians and their ideas, church history, biblical studies and exegesis,

---

[1] Leonard Sweet, *Rings of Fire: Walking in Faith through a Volcanic Future* (Colorado Springs: NavPress, 2019), 186.

and a large sample of other areas but little of how these are to relate to the life and mission of the church today.

Fourth, many seminaries remain out of touch with the needs and desires of students interested in pursuing ministry today. Increasingly students are unwilling or unable (or both) to uproot and take on several years of graduate study. Many are already engaged in active ministry and looking not to leave this for graduate school but to gain the tools, insights, and skills needed to serve more effectively in their context.

Fifth, theological education has become prohibitively expensive.[1] The high cost of facilities, personnel, and countless other expenses require significant income, which all but inevitably affects tuition.

Obviously, these are broad brush strokes. They may describe some institutions (or seasons within them) with considerable accuracy and others only barely. Nevertheless, one may arguably hold that such characteristics remain sufficiently common and influential across theological education today to justify a courageous and critical assessment of the current state of theological education in hopes buttressing priceless foundations that must not be allowed to fall.

Repairing Broken Foundations

The problems befalling Winchester Cathedral had been growing for centuries before William Walker was

---

[1] Using data available from Association for Theological Schools (ATS) and looking at twenty of the most well-known seminaries the cost of tuition and fees for one year averaged $26,605. ATS reports that the average debt in 2018 of those needing student loans for their seminary degree was $32,817. https://web.archive.org/web/20160101000000*/ https://www.ats.edu/files/galleries/current-data-on-educational-debt -among-ats-graduates-aug-2018.pdf.

brought in to build a new foundation. The large cracks described at the turn of the twentieth century began centuries earlier, crescive and inexorable fractures inching across both years and walls. There is little doubt that through these years repairs were made. Cracks were patched, stones returned to places from which they had fallen, and paint applied. And the bulging walls and slowly sinking buildings? Likely they were largely ignored, either in hope (or denial) that the situation would not get worse or in hopelessness that it could not be made better.

But there comes a time when it becomes broadly evident that the magnitude of the problems can no longer be solved with plaster and paint. What is needed is a courageous and creative rebuilding of the foundations to support the structure into the future.[1]

There is no doubt that seminaries need to "re-engineer" their methods. This does not mean "dumb it all down" or abandon academic depth for populist relevancy or tradition for cultural pablum. It does not mean turning the seminaries into religious trade schools. The task is to do theological education in a way consistent with the foundations we have been given while freshly supporting these in ways that enhance the purpose of the structure for the work it was meant to do. Leonard Sweet describes what might look like:

> The issue is not that seminaries are "too academic." The issue is that seminaries need new academics, a new model of academe that will make sense of what is going on around us based on what went on in the past, explore what the impact of change has been before and will be

---

[1] A wonderful study on this theme is Ted A. Smith, *The End of Theological Education* (Grand Rapids: Eerdmans, 2023). This book is part of a profoundly helpful series entitled Theological Education between the times.

now, and suggest preparations that will enable the church to adapt. Just as the culture needs public intellectuals, the church needs public theologians who will write in the vernacular and not cast out the colloquial.[1]

Restoring Foundations

What might a new model of academe look like? What emphases might we take up or restore to support the ancient walls?[2] These are obviously huge questions that involve far more than "patching" the cracks. The breadth of possible tasks, approaches, and areas of focus are numerous and require more time and space than available. With this limitation, let me suggest further "broad brush strokes" that I believe are vital to rebuilding the foundations of theological education.

First, we must restore a strong emphasis upon the spiritual growth and maturity of our students. The spiritual life is not a private or personal element of the pastor's life. It is not something distinct or isolated from the work of ministry. It is the foundational element of all ministry practices and leadership. For this reason, we must restore a priority on cultivating the spiritual depth of our students

---

[1] Leonard Sweet, "The Decline and Fall of Seminaries," *Rings of Fire: Walking in Faith through a Volcanic Future* (Colorado Springs: NavPress, 2019), 185.

[2] It is deeply encouraging to see many working on such questions. Perry Shaw's *Transforming Theological Education: A Practical Handbook for Integrative Learning* (2nd ed.; Carlisle, Cumbria: Langham Publishing, 2022) is profoundly helpful and insightful. The series Theological Education Between the Times (Eerdmans), consisting of at least nine volumes, courageously looks at the state of theological education today, including important areas unmentioned in this summary, and provides creative and helpful insights for all seeking to make theological education the best it can be.

and relentlessly endeavor to show how spiritual life, academic insights, and ministry practices can and must intertwine.

Historically, seminaries have focused upon the academic credentials of its faculty with little emphasis upon their understanding of and participation in the life and ministry of the local parish. But one must ask: how can one with little or no experience in the daily life and ministry of a congregation prepare students to be its leaders? How can a seminary, effectively disconnected from the life and mission of the church, prepare a new generation of pastors to shepherd it? At the Flourish Institute of Theology, we require that everyone teaching for us not only have the appropriate academic credentials. But with this, we require they also have been, and remain, deeply involved in the ministry life of the local parish. Even more, we call upon our teachers to constantly look at how to take the deep ideas of Scripture, theology, and history and apply them to the questions, needs, hurts, and lives of people filling the church each Sunday and the culture in which the church is placed.

Seminary, at its best, must include the best of the life of the church. That is to say that our classes and academic life together should look like the church at its best and healthiest. This is different than the norms of the last decades which tended to shape seminary community and life primarily around the classroom and the educative process. This is, of course, a vital and real element of seminary. But we hold that community must include more than this. Instead, we seek to build genuine community between our students and between students and faculty. We seek to show and reflect in the life of our seminary community the best of life in the church. We seek to build up one another, carry one another's burdens, challenge each other, and push each other ever closer to a Christ-shaped life. This deep community is built through regular classes held online, availability of teachers to students, pastoral care, and a network of small groups that go deep in both academic reflection and care and prayer for one another.

The most far-reaching agent for change has been the internet and the ability to offer online classes and community that is deep, accessible, and affordable. Tools such as online platforms for running classes, keeping in contact with students, and building community combined with libraries such as the Digital Theological library allow a depth of unprecedented access to astonishing educational resources. While not perfect and not without problems, online education provides a new and all but unlimited means of expanding and improving theological education. It is incumbent upon us though, to critically and creatively engage with this new medium, inventing and designing the appropriate pedagogies that can bring excellence and depth to our educative processes. What is required is new wineskins for new wine.

Without denying the difficulties before us (the metaphorical bowed walls, cracks, bogs, and dark, cold depths) there is every reason to believe that these can be addressed and overcome, and the priceless structure be made to rest afresh on solid foundations. That so many are creatively engaged in precisely this goal inspires great hope for the future of theological education.

Mark Patterson is the founding President of the Flourish Institute of Theology, a Graduate School of Ministry. Mark has led the design of our programs, classes, and curriculum. He recruits and trains our faculty and teaches in the areas of theology, church history, and pastoral ministry. Mark earned his BA degree in theology from Whitworth University, an MDiv degree from Princeton Theological Seminary, and a PhD in theology from King's College London. He has been a pastor for over 45 years and an adjunct professor of theology for Gordon-Conwell Theological Seminary and Fuller Theological Seminary.

Flourish Institute of Theology: A Graduate School of Ministry was as new seminary created in 2021 by the Covenant Order of Evangelical Presbyterians (ECO). It was designed from the very start to offer not just an outstanding theological education under the best teachers possible, but theological education shaped for ministry service in ministry. Our School of Ministry is committed to training pastors and ministry leaders who are deeply steeped in biblical and theological insights. We aim to train our students to be theological thinkers who are then released to creatively, winsomely, and powerfully proclaim the message of the Gospel within the church and our twenty-first century culture.

The Ministry of Listening

Juliet Mousseau

Over the past five years, the Catholic Church under the leadership of Pope Francis (and now Pope Leo) has begun a shift toward communal leadership, in the form of synodality. Church synods started in the apostolic age, with the Council of Jerusalem. Church leadership came together to address issues of fundamental importance to the church community and its practices. Throughout the two millennia following that first council, the Catholic Church eventually established a synod system that included only the bishops. In fact, the Vatican formally calls this practice of regular meetings of Church leadership the Synod of Bishops, even as non-bishops are now invited to participate and vote in the meetings.

While the changes at the top of the hierarchical structure of the church are amazing to behold, their impact on the day-to-day ministry of local diocesan and parish communities has widely varied, especially in the United States. Ideally, synodality will become a way of listening to the voices of all the faithful as decisions are being made at all levels of the Church. It is a radical challenge to the historical hierarchical structure of the Church. In some dioceses (including my own) ordinary parishioners are being trained to practice synodality in parish councils. The intention is that the local community will fully embrace the mission of their parish and determine its direction. While the Catholic hierarchy remains fully in place, ordained ministers are being called on to act in concert with what they hear from their people.

The process of synodal decision-making is clearly laid out in the official documents available online.[1] As Pope Francis described it:

> It is an exercise in mutual listening, conducted at all levels of the Church and involving the entire People of God. The Cardinal Vicar, the auxiliary bishops, priests, religious and laity have to listen to one another, and then to everyone else. Listening, speaking and listening. It is not about garnering opinions, not a survey, but a matter of listening to the Holy Spirit.... (*Address of the Holy Father to the Faithful of the Diocese of Rome*, 18 September 2021).

Drawing on the term itself, Pope Francis speaks of the process as "journeying together," reiterating the horizontal nature of human relationships and their importance for the church. The act of listening to others, including those we disagree with, fosters a spirit of belonging and welcome to a church that can sometimes be seen as unwelcoming. Synodality can be a way forward in the polarized world and Church in which we find ourselves today.

While this is a new era in the Roman Catholic church, the principles of synodality have been present in our ministerial education for a long time. Pastoral sensitivity begins with a deep belief that the image and likeness of God is present in every human being and that God's hand can be seen in all that God creates. Human beings were made holy, with profound dignity inherent in their very being. The Franciscan School of Theology, in training lay and to-be-ordained ministers, emphasizes the

---

[1] https://web.archive.org/web/20250000000000*/synod.va

fundamental goodness of the human person and all of creation. Taking seriously God's reflection at the end of each day of creation: "And he saw that it was (very) good," (Gen 1) ministry means seeing the goodness in each person and listening to the voice of God in their lives and needs. Emphasizing human goodness does not deny the reality of sin and evil, but it does put it in perspective. Yes, human beings sin. However, God's goodness can never be overcome by human sinfulness. Human beings are always good at their core.

The ministry of listening holds space for witnessing the goodness within each human person. Recognition and a sense of belonging through presence and listening contribute deeply to healing the divisions and polarization that exist in the world. In the words of St. Francis of Assisi, affirmed by Pope Francis, we are all brothers and sisters to one another, *Fratelli tutti*. May the practice of synodality and deep listening remind all of us of our common humanity and our shared image of God within.

Juliet Mousseau, RSCJ, PhD, is a Religious of the Sacred Heart of Jesus. She serves as the Vice President for Academic Affairs at the Franciscan School of Theology in San Diego, California. She is also a professor of historical theology specializing in the Middle Ages.

The **Franciscan School of Theology** is a graduate school of theology that prepares men and women, lay and religious, for ministry. Guided and governed in its educational mission, community life, and degree programs by the Order of Friars Minor (Franciscans), the Franciscan School brings the questions of contemporary culture, society, and Church into dialog with the ever-ancient and ever-new Word of the Gospel.

Is (Theological) Education a Waste of Time?

Enoh Šeba

I still vividly remember when, about thirty years ago, a professor of mine wryly remarked, "Education is wasted on the young!" At the time, I thought it was an unusual and perhaps provocative thing for a theologian to say, given that he made a living teaching mostly young people. I was ready to attribute it to his peculiar sense of humor.

Today, however, this claim has become almost common knowledge. Churches and denominations in different parts of the world struggle to attract new ministerial candidates. Young Christians rarely consider a degree in theology a promising path for their professional development. Even when they are willing to contribute to their local congregations or bring a Christian perspective to their professional lives, they don't see investing two or three years in a proper theological degree as an attractive option like they did in the past.

In fact, this may only be a small part of a much bigger problem. Although there are regional differences, many of us are painfully aware that traditional academic theological education is constantly losing its appeal. Theological schools and institutions have a hard time convincing ministers with little or no previous theological training to invest in continuous education to support their ministries, prevent stagnation, and address the ever-changing challenges of the contemporary world. This difficulty is further intensified in situations where churches are traditionally suspicious of academic theology, viewing it as detached and useless "in the field." At universities that once had divinity schools or departments of theology, where proper theology was taught, we now find only religious studies or the comparative study of religion.

These problems are enough to make one wonder if the question in the title should be reformulated as, "Is theological education a waste of time?" I am convinced that answering this question requires us to first consider another question: "What kind of theological education?" In a sense, the need for theological training is as strong as ever. However, for this need to be recognized and met competently, we, as theological educators, must be ready to reassess our approach to theological education. What I am going to suggest is not radically new or unheard of. Various high-quality programs and courses have already been developed around the world, taking all these concerns into account. This is only a brief summary of features that present-day theological education should incorporate to be worthy of people's time and resources.

Make It Lifelong

The distinction between formal and informal education is more blurred than ever. Although formal, accredited degrees remain valuable and are considered a hallmark of theological education, more and more people recognize the growing importance of short-term, informal training programs that don't require formal qualifications. This makes theological education more accessible and approachable, even for those without extensive theological knowledge acquired during their professional development. At the same time, these programs create opportunities for people to continue learning well into later stages of life, ensuring that theological education is not just for the young. This is particularly advantageous as churches recognize the contributions of their older members. These members may not be full-time ministerial staff, but they maintain a teachable attitude and are open to new knowledge, experiences, and skills. This shift must be embraced, yet some educational institutions still need to adjust and stop treating non-degree programs and short-term courses as inferior.

Welcome Flexibility and Contextuality

It does not take much discernment or extensive research to conclude that we live in a world affected by rapid and unprecedented changes. During your lifetime, each of you has probably witnessed several major cultural shifts, experienced more than a few global crises, and seen interfaith dynamics undergo repeated transformation. The Christian presence and mission require a response to these developments, and theological education plays an indispensable role in articulating these responses.

The problem is that most theological degrees, which take several years to complete, are not flexible enough to accommodate the speed of the changes students face. It usually takes time to change and then re-accredit undergraduate or graduate programs. By the time this process is finished, new needs and challenges may have arisen. This is why shorter, more flexible programs and courses, which do not require complex academic procedures to launch and implement, can be a welcome addition to existing, more traditional degrees.

This sense of flexibility may also allow individual students to create a curriculum that fits their needs and limited resources, better equipping them to adapt their ministry and witness to new realities. Moreover, adaptability in designing such an education opens the door to highly contextualized content. Despite the strong influence of globalization, local conditions remain a key factor in the successful development of practical and sustainable solutions, and theological education is no exception. Teaching theology while being anchored in a contextual positionality greatly increases the likelihood of passing on competencies that will help students be culturally relevant and identity-conscious. Additionally, learning opportunities that allow students to remain engaged with their professional, social, church, and family contexts (as opposed to full-time studies that involve physical detachment from these contexts) mean that acquired knowledge can be tested and evaluated constantly in real-life settings.

Implement Adult Learning Theory

The field of educational theories of learning is indeed fascinating. Each one has its own advantages and merits. However, when it comes to shaping contemporary forms of theological education, I believe that special attention should be given to andragogy. There are several reasons for this.

First, as previously mentioned, most participants in educational processes are adults. As such, their self-concept is typically well-developed, as opposed to that of children (or even young adults). This has at least two consequences: Adult students can participate in directing their own learning process, and they can find internal motivation. Second, adult students (especially those older ones) have a wealth of experience to draw from. Often, they are heavily invested in the subject matter and readily contribute their existing knowledge and experience. Third, when they decide to return to education, they are ready to learn, but they look for practical approaches. Their desire to learn usually stems from issues related to work, their personal life, or church/community-related ministry. Finally, these people are not interested in memorizing content; rather, they are interested in solving real-life problems.

Adult learning theory should not be applied as a one-size-fits-all solution to all educational needs. However, its principles can certainly be used to develop more effective modes of learning for actively engaged adult students.

Preserve Communal and Formative Dimension

Historically, Christian education has been understood as nurturing learning communities where individuals receive academic knowledge and experience spiritual formation. Maintaining this emphasis may be much more challenging in today's educational landscape, where remote and online learning opportunities abound. Although previous recommendations may seem to encourage an individualized or even individualistic approach to theological education, I firmly believe that it is crucial not to forget that the Christian faith must always be explored in community. Students need each other to engage in dialogue. To sharpen one another's understanding, they must deliberately make their inquiry a shared one. To hear diverse voices, they need opportunities to listen to others. To be formed by their learning, students need humility in relation to their peers. All of this becomes possible only if educators intentionally build and sustain a space in which a community of learners can thrive.

Although the question "*Is theological education a waste of time?*" may seem pressing or even unsettling, I think we will do better if we focus our energy on another question: "*What kind of education?*" It would be unrealistic to expect this question to be settled quickly and then left behind. In fact, it is more likely that Christian educators will have to engage with it over the long term. However, it is only through ongoing grappling with this question that theological exploration will remain vibrant and relevant as new matters and contexts emerge.

Here at the International Baptist Theological Study Centre in Amsterdam, we often tell our doctoral students that we are not a PhD factory. By this, we mean at least two things. Firstly, theological education is something that is inherently organic and ever-changing for us and is subject to the trials brought about by living in the contemporary world. Secondly, we believe that education is about the growth and maturity of the whole person, as well as their communities. I am deeply convinced that, as long as we adhere to these principles, theological education will never be a waste of any resource.

The International Baptist Theological Study Centre (IBTS) is a theological research community and training network serving the European Baptist Federation (covering Europe, the Middle East, and Central Asia) and the wider Baptist community. Originally founded in 1949, it first operated in Rüschlikon, Switzerland, before moving to Prague. In 2014, it relocated to Amsterdam. There, it collaborates with the School of Religion and Theology (SRT) at the Faculty of Social Sciences and Humanities at Vrije Universiteit Amsterdam. The IBTS specialises in doctoral training, research and leadership development in the fields of Baptist identity, mission and practice, while maintaining a robust research library and an international community of scholars.

Dr. Enoh Šeba has been Director of the IBTS in Amsterdam since 1 September 2024. Originally from Zagreb in Croatia, Šeba holds a PhD from Spurgeon's College (University of Chester) and previously earned his master's degree at IBTS. Prior to this, he served for two decades as Secretary and Assistant Professor in Practical Theology at the Faculty of Theology Matthias Flacius Illyricus at the University of Zagreb, where he taught courses in homiletics, liturgics, research methodology and more. During this time, he also directed empirical studies of Protestant minority congregations in Croatia. His current research interests focus on preaching, particularly bridging the gap between preacher and listener, liturgical innovation, and the practical expressions of Christian unity, combining empirical methods with theological reflection.

Reflections on the Banalization of Knowledge
On AI and Anicent Oral Culture

Suheil Laher

"New lamps for old!" Abanazar, the wicked sorcerer in the classic Aladdin fictional tale, was counting on humans' penchant for what is new in order to recover the old yet valuable magic lamp. New does not necessarily mean better, and indeed, as Rudyard Kipling's poem "New Lamps" reminds us, the call to replace the ancient is sometimes inspired by the devil. With the Artificial Intelligence (AI) revolution now underway, it behoves us as theological educators to pause to reflect on the pros and cons of this amazing new development. As a representative of a Muslim seminary in the DTL community of mostly Christian institutions, I felt it appropriate to share some reflections on libraries, AI, and education, reflections that are informed by the fifteen-century tradition of Muslim (Islamic) scholarship.

We should remind ourselves that this is not the first revolution involving the mechanics of transmitting knowledge. Oral transmission was the norm for many early societies, including that of seventh-century Arabia into which was born Muhammad, the last prophet of Islam (Muslims acknowledge all God's Prophets, including Noah, Abraham, and Moses, with Jesus also being one of the greatest prophets). The Prophet Muhammad, himself unlettered, promoted literacy among his followers, and had scribes write down the Quran, his revelation from God. His immediate followers disagreed among themselves on whether to write down the Prophet's own words (the *hadith*), based on several factors, one of which may have been deprecation for the written over the oral and fear of the memory becoming dulled. A millennium earlier, the Greek philosopher Socrates had disapproved of writing for this very reason. Although an effective consensus emerged among Muslim scholars within a couple of generations about the desirability of writing, oral transmission of religious knowledge from a righteous teacher was still considered more privileged. The renowned Cordoban Maliki judge Ibn Rushd (d. 1126, grandfather of the philosopher Averroes) remarked, "In the early age, knowledge was in the hearts of men, and thereafter it was transcribed onto the skins of animals, but the keys to it remained in the hearts of men." Even after the hadiths were compiled into books, the contents of the books were transmitted orally, a practice that has continued even into the present.

The American Jesuit scholar Walter Ong (d. 2003) has written at length about the pros and cons of orality and writing and also discussed how the ascendance of writing (and later the printing press) restructured human consciousness. He observed that writing facilitates abstract thought and precision, at the expense of detachment from emotions and lived experience. This observation serves as a reminder to me, as a Muslim theological educator, of the tension between dispassionate and emotionally on the one hand and ideologically-invested scholarship on the other hand. We religious academics need to navigate this tension with care. The availability of a plethora of books and other resources, such as those facilitated by DTL, has the potential to be a curse or a blessing. We need to avoid the temptation of confirmation bias, sometimes on the pretext of concentrating on digging one's own confessional well. Through reading different and opposing perspectives, we can open ourselves to questioning our assumptions, soul-searching, and continually refining our understanding of God and the world. A Muslim sage has said, "Humility is to accept the truth regardless of who is saying it." As a Muslim (once again), I have benefitted from reading the work of authors from different confessional backgrounds, which has allowed me to better understand common ground, parallels, and differences. Judaism, Christianity, and Islam have particularly strong connections and much common ground, which we should encourage our students to explore and celebrate.

In oral societies, memory tends to be stronger. Based on the privileging of the oral that was the norm in the Muslim scholarly tradition, students traditionally often memorized didactic poems, and even prose texts before (or in parallel with) learning their detailed explanation. There are definite benefits to memorization as a pedagogical tool, but also potential pitfalls. Among the benefits are exercising and developing the brain, and I fear that unbridled use of AI is threatening this, with increasing numbers of students using AI to write essays, and even professors using AI to summarize articles. A recent MIT study (even though it is not yet peer-reviewed), which was discussed in a *Time* magazine article by Andrew Chow, found that even though AI might increase productivity and efficiency, it reduces people's motivation and intellectual engagement. The study suggests that long-term use of AI leads to poorer memory of one's AI-assisted output and is detrimental to critical thinking. I am reminded of Oscar Wilde's words:

> *"Oho!" they cried, "The world is wide,*
> *But fettered limbs go lame!"*[1]

Brain atrophy is a terrifying thought, especially in the Muslim theological context of the moral obligation to give thanks to God by making good use of the organs and tools we have been given. One might rejoin that freeing the brain from this work allows us to direct our efforts to other, more lofty things. That may be the case, and remains to be seen, but there is still the danger that many will simply use AI for shortcuts and not go any further.

Another danger of unchecked attachment to technology is loneliness and boredom, and during the Covid pandemic we witnessed a rise in mental health issues, especially among the young. As I have mentioned, knowledge was usually conveyed through face-to-face interaction in the Muslim scholarly tradition, especially in the earlier centuries. The student of sacred knowledge would typically study first from the scholars of their locality and then travel to other cities and lands to acquire knowledge from the learned men there. Such travel (termed the *riḥla*), was an integral part of scholarly life across the disciplines. One would not be taken seriously as a scholar without having traveled in pursuit of knowledge. Benefits of the *riḥla* include broadening one's horizons, developing as a person (including learning resilience through enduring the toils and troubles of travel), and learning morals and good etiquette through interaction with righteous teachers.

As I reflect on the easy access to knowledge in the digital age, I cannot help but be concerned that today's students (especially with the advent of AI) might not fully

---

[1] The Ballad of Reading Gaol" https://web.archive.org/web/20160101000000*/http://www.ricorso.net/rx/library/authors/classic/Wilde_O/poetry/Ballad.htm

appreciate the value and sacredness of knowledge; "easy come, easy go," as the adage goes. Technology, and especially AI, has contributed to a banalization of knowledge. The effortlessness with which we often acquire knowledge in the digital age is a problem now exacerbated by the re-packaging of existing knowledge by AI. This can be partially countered by reminding our students that true knowledge is that which is put into action for the betterment of one's self (including having a better connection with the Creator) and the world. As the early ascetic Hasan al-Basri (d. 728) said, "Knowledge is of two [sorts]: Knowledge [solely] on the tongue is God's proof against the son of Adam, [whereas] knowledge [internalized in] the heart is the beneficial [type of] knowledge."

AI is likely here to stay, but I proffer that we as theological educators have the duty to keep reminding our students to harness the myriad digital reading materials wisely, by sincere and deep engagement with the material, avoiding the tendency to use AI for shortcuts. I would also stress the importance of the human dimension, not only mere interaction but also the inculcation of morals, which is an essential part of the seminarian's training. We know not what the future will bring, whether for us or for our students, but we can hope and pray that we benefit from the new without losing out on the benefits of the ancient and time-tested.

Suheil Laher: Suheil Laher is Assistant Professor of Islamic Studies and Lead Faculty at Boston Islamic Seminary, and Faculty Associate in Quranic Studies at Hartford International University. He previously served as Academic Dean at Fawakih Institute for Classical Arabic (where he remains a Senior Curriculum Advisor), and before that as Muslim Chaplain at the Massachusetts Institute of Technology. He received an MA in Religious Studies from Boston University, and a PhD in Near Eastern Languages and Civilizations from Harvard University. He also has *ijazahs* (traditional authorizations) in Islamic theology, Islamic law, hadith and other Islamic disciplines. His publications include a book (*Tawātur in Islamic Thought Transmission, Certitude and Orthodoxy*, Edinburgh University Press, 2024), as well as a number of journal articles, review essays, and book reviews.

Boston Islamic Seminary: The mission of the Boston Islamic Seminary (BIS) is to prepare exemplary and professional Muslim American religious leaders for compassionate service to society. The vision was conceived in 2008, and BIS officially became a legal entity in 2015. Since then, BIS has offered a variety of educational programs for adult learners, including a Continuing Education Program, Professional Development Certificates, Workshops, fellowships, and public book talks. A significant milestone was achieved in December 2020 when the Massachusetts Board of Higher Education (MABHE) granted BIS the authority to award a Master in Islamic Religious Leadership (MIRL) degree. This made BIS the first institution in the United States to offer such a degree.

The Wisdom of the Ages and of Age

Ora Horn Prouser

Traditionally, people decide to be ordained as rabbis or cantors early in life, and many begin seminary studies immediately after college. There is great value in this. They begin the challenging curriculum of rabbinical or cantorial training while still in college or early graduate school mode, entrenched in the academic cycle and structure, and are able to anticipate long careers serving the Jewish People. At the same time, it means that they serve individuals and communities seeking wisdom and support during both happy and sad times of life without really having personally experienced much of life. Many begin officiating at funerals after having attended very few funerals themselves, and perhaps not having experienced death in their own immediate families. Similarly, they provide premarital counseling while living single, or having been married for a short time. While I appreciate that this is a perfectly legitimate and powerful way to start one's career in the clergy, it means that the young rabbi will gain their life experience while already serving their community.

At the Academy for Jewish Religion, a pluralistic Jewish seminary and graduate school, our students have been primarily second and third career for most of our almost seventy year history. While we do have some students in their twenties, the majority of our students range in age from their thirties through their seventies. We have students who begin their clergy training after retiring from full careers in other fields. While some are studying simply for their own enjoyment, the majority of our students are studying in order to serve. They come to their studies and their places of employment with a wealth of life experience that is rich and varied. They have celebrated and mourned; they have worked in professional careers; they have learned from all the people they have engaged with over the years; they have seen many different ways of living. They have a better understanding of the diversity of the human experience and bring all of that into their work. At the same time, they take the same curriculum as our younger students, needing to learn the same amount of Hebrew, sacred literature, and everything else included in the prescribed course of study.

While it may seem unusual to have second career students -- in fact they are often called "nontraditional students" -- beginning a career at an advanced age is actually embedded in Jewish tradition. Rabbi Akiva, a rabbi of the first through second century CE, famously began studying at the age of forty. He then became one of the most important rabbis of the early rabbinic period. He was an uneducated man before he came to begin sacred learning, needing to start at the very beginning, and learned to read along with his children. The story is told that he saw how water could wear away stone, and deduced from that fact that constant and intense effort can lead to any achievement. He thus became a model of the persistence, dedication, and work necessary to one who comes to learning at a later stage in life. At the same time, he is a model of the rewards of that effort and hard work.

Lest we think that Rabbi Akiva is the only such model, we only need to look to the Torah to see that Moses began his career at the age of eighty. At that advanced age he first began the job of leading the Israelites, and serving as God's prophet. Moses felt ill-equipped to be that leader, as we see from his responses at the burning bush, claiming that he did not have what was needed to be that leader. He claimed that he did not have the standing, the knowledge base, the power, the talent, or the speaking ability to lead the Israelites. Yet, God assured Moses that he did have what he needed, as God, and then his brother Aaron, would be with him as support and assistance. The point was that while Moses felt inadequate and ill-equipped, God was secure in the choice of Moses and knew that he could make it happen. Similarly, we see with our students who come to us at more advanced ages, they may be concerned about perceived deficits, but we see the talent, the passion, the strength, and the ability. Sometimes we play the role of Aaron, helping them to achieve what they did not think they could.

We have learned a lot about adult learners over the years, and how we can help them to achieve their dreams. For example, they need to continue to feel that they are always being treated as adults with respect and trust reflecting their maturity and sophistication. We need to remember that each of these individuals has a full life outside of school including family, professional commitments, and communal responsibilities, and they need to know that we understand that. Sometimes we have to pay attention to physical situations such as attention to size of print, the uses of microphones and hearing devices, and additional technological support. In addition, they need to see the importance of the work they are doing and how it will be relevant to their work.

Of course there is more, but the most important conclusion we have reached is that the Jewish world is exceedingly enriched through the service of those who come to clergy training as a second or third career. The Torah concludes by observing that "Never again did there arise in Israel a prophet like Moses" (Deuteronomy 34:10). Still, every rabbi traces her or his ordination back to that peerless leader. Adult learners and second career clergy can, further, identify in Moses a reassuring precedent for their own professional and religious journeys.

Dr. Ora Horn Prouser is the Executive Director and Academic Dean of the Academy for Jewish Religion. She earned her bachelor's and doctoral degrees from the Jewish Theological Seminary, as well as a bachelor's degree from Columbia University. She has published extensively on the Bible, focusing on disability studies, gender, and literary analysis. Her book *Esau's Blessing: How the Bible Embraces Those with Special Needs* was a finalist for the National Jewish Book Council Award in 2012 and won the Gold Medal at the 2016 Special Needs Book Awards. Her book *Under One Tent: Circus, Judaism, and Bible* breaks new ground in its use of movement and circus arts in the study of the biblical text. Her most recent books, which she co-edited (*Seder Interrupted: A Post–October 7 Haggadah Supplement*, *These Holy Days: A High Holy Days Supplement After October 7*, *An Upside-Down World: Esther and Antisemitism*, and *Perhaps There Is Hope: A Tisha B'Av Supplement*), are among her latest publications. They invite us to wrestle with the Jewish holidays in the world after October 7.

The Academy for Jewish Religion (AJR) enables qualified candidates from all geographies, life situations, and perspectives within Jewish life to become clergy serving the Jewish community. The school's flexibility and personalized approach, combined with its accredited academic rigor, serve a wide range of students and have led AJR to embrace pluralism as an active verb. We value difference and the opportunity to experience it deeply and meaningfully. We train our clergy to engage actively with one another, with Jewish traditions, and with the world, in order to lead with deep intention, curiosity, and openness to shared learning.

Part III

Innovations in Theological Education and Formation

New experiments in theological education are already underway. Educators and institutions are testing alternative models, creative practices, and emerging tools in the hope of serving students and communities more effectively. The essays in this section explore those innovations, drawing from practical experience as well as hopeful imagination. The aim is not to prescribe a single path forward but to encourage readers to learn from what is being tried and to carry the spirit of experimentation into their own contexts.

Ready, Fire, Aim
Information Gathering and Decision-Making in Uncertain Times

Thomas E. Phillips

In my role as executive director of the DTL, I work with a lot of seminary administrators. If my observation of these hard-working, dedicated professionals has taught me anything, it is simply this: Seminary administrators live in a world of accelerating change. Financial pressures, enrollment fluctuations, cultural shifts, and technological disruption mean that the seas administrators navigated even a few years ago are no longer the same. Amid such volatility, older models of slow, lengthy and drawn-out decision-making are simply not viable. This essay explores an information gathering and decision-making process appropriate for the contemporary landscape of theological education.

A Tale of the DTL

By most measures, the DTL has been a story of success and growth—both institutionally and missionally. The DTL was formed in 2016 and initially served two seminaries. In the spring of 2025, the DTL served as the primary—and typically the only—library for just over 100 seminaries in developed nations and for several times that number in developing nations. It also serves thousands of individual religious professionals in North America through its Seminary BookShelf and hundreds of thousands more researchers globally through its Open Access DTL.

The DTL manages the world's largest collection of digital content in religious studies, providing its members, even very, very small schools, with a world class research library in the field. The DTL is also now establishing its own publishing house.

When asked how the DTL was able to create such a successful institution in the shrinking industry of theological education, I always answer the same way: I work with some really great people (the DTL now has 10 employees) and we practice the philosophy of "Ready, Fire, Aim."

Rather than the traditional "Ready, Aim, Fire" model, a model which emphasizes preparation and precision before action, the DTL believes that effective leadership in today's environment demands a willingness to act decisively once the preponderance of evidence suggests the wisdom (or necessity) of a certain course of action even in the face of acknowledged uncertainty. After taking such initial action, leaders can fine-tune their strategies based on real-time feedback and shifting realities. "Ready, Fire, Aim."

The Information Cycle in Decision-Making

Everyone wants to make sound, data-driven decisions. That means gathering information and acting on that information in a manner consistent with the institution's mission and values. Assuming the institution's mission and values are clear, *the hard part of the process is knowing how much information is enough.*

Let's consider the pandemic lesson. Well before the pandemic, most academics understood that the internet and its associated technologies were going to change educational delivery systems. Everyone at seminaries, denominational officials and accreditation agencies was talking about these changes, and thinking about these changes, and talking about these changes, and thinking about these changes, and talking about... However, real, substantial change was rare. Then came the pandemic and profound changes occurred literally within a matter of days.

The pandemic lesson should be clear: It doesn't take that long to effect massive change. The problem is nearly always a matter of inadequate determination, not inadequate understanding or limited capacity. The problem is almost never insufficient information.

I. Ready
The Myth of Complete Information

Leaders who crave complete information before taking action are like the person who says, "Ready, aim... aim... aim... aim..." but who never fires. Their endless hesitation creates a stagnant environment where nothing ever really changes (it is always possible to credibly claim that one does not yet have all the data). This constant state of preparation, without resolution, exhausts the energy of innovators and ultimately drives change agents to leave in frustration. *When decisions are perpetually deferred, the institution loses its most dynamic thinkers, who are the very people most capable of leading it into the future. Indecision can be the coward's way of avoiding responsibility and accountability.*

Administrators are often paralyzed by the fear of acting without perfect and complete knowledge. This paralysis-by-analysis, or what some call "decision inertia," stems from the mistaken belief that successful decisions require exhaustive data. In reality, waiting for all the information rarely leads to better outcomes. Instead, the avoidance of change often causes institutions to miss strategic windows of opportunity and simply to fail in familiar ways. *Failing in familiar and comfortable ways is still failing.*

In practice, the pursuit of complete information leads to endless meetings, prolonged studies, repetitious analyses, delayed actions, and an ever-growing sense of institutional stagnation. By the time a decision is finally made, opportunities have passed, resources have been wasted and mission effectiveness has been forfeited. In fact, the context may have changed so dramatically that the decision is no longer relevant. The target moved while during the aiming process.

Indeed, in seasons of rapid change, the greatest danger is not making the wrong decision but failing to make any decision at all. Indecision breeds institutional drift, undermines morale, and sends a message of uncertainty and fear. In fast-moving contexts, the costs of hesitation can far exceed the consequences of a misstep. The courage to act decisively is often what separates thriving institutions from those in decline.

The Principle of the Preponderance of Evidence

The solution is not to abandon evidence-based leadership but to recalibrate what constitutes "enough" evidence. Seminary leaders must become comfortable acting on a preponderance of evidence. This means *acting on probabilities, not certainties,* a tipping of the scales, not absolute proof.

When the available data, stakeholder input, and contextual realities suggest that a certain direction is probably wise, leaders must consider themselves "ready." They must then be willing to "fire," that is, to make the decision, implement the initiative, or begin the new strategy.

As leaders move closer to the likelihood of a particular course of action, their approach to evidence gathering should shift. Early in the decision-making process, it is natural to seek supportive evidence that builds the case for taking action. *But as the decision becomes increasingly compelling, the role of evidence should transition from justification to falsification.* Leaders should begin asking not, "Why should we do this?" but rather, "Is there any compelling reason why we should not do this?"

This mindset shift toward falsification ensures that administrators are not blindsided by predictable problems. Good decision-making anticipates counterarguments, addresses potential risks, and incorporates safeguards. It is not enough to build a strong case in favor of action; leaders must actively seek out evidence that could invalidate or significantly challenge the proposed course. If no such counterevidence emerges (or if only minor and manageable complications are found), then the leader can move forward with greater confidence, prepared for mid-course corrections. When the decision-makers can find no compelling reason to delay action, it is time to act. Fire!

To be clear, a focused attempt to falsify one's theory, to refute one's own opinion or demonstrate the folly of a preferred course of action is not the same thing as giving heed to "nay sayers." There will never be a shortage of skeptics who prefer the familiar to the unfamiliar. Instead, this shift toward falsification is a guard against group think and premature consensus. Still, at some point, the objections become known and can be accommodated, negated, accounted for or even dismissed (everyone told us that the idea behind the DTL, the idea of a co-owned all digital library, would never work, but our founding team found ways around the obstacles).

Look for enough positive evidence, then seek out the counterevidence, then act. *If the positive evidence is compelling and the counterevidence isn't strong enough to veto the proposed course of action, it is time to act.*

II. Fire
Action as the First Step in Discernment

Taking action (firing) is not the end of decision-making; it is the beginning of authentic discernment. While theoretical planning is valuable, nothing reveals the practical strengths and weaknesses of a strategy more effectively than its real-world application. People learn by doing. Implementation exposes gaps in logic, reveals unforeseen variables, and clarifies what truly works in context.

The temptation to keep refining a plan indefinitely is very real. Every institution has its limitations in terms of time, resources, and energy. *Leaders should understand that no amount of pre-action theorizing will match the speed and depth of insight gained through implementation.* Provisional action often teaches more in a week than meetings and white papers can reveal in a year.

By enacting a preliminary plan, administrators place themselves in the best position to observe outcomes, solicit feedback, and make informed refinements. It is only in motion that strategies can be steered. Thus, the act of firing is not a commitment to perfection but a disciplined step into the realm of learning and realignment.

I have a billionaire friend who works in tech. He often tells his team, "Do it once for me." He understands that people learn by doing; doing a thing one time makes each future iteration more efficient… or it demonstrates the folly of repeating failure. Either way, progress is made.

III. Aim
Mid-Course Corrections: The Power of Adaptive Leadership

In the "Ready, Fire, Aim" philosophy, this stage of correction and adjustment represents the crucial third step: Aim. It is here that initial insights and bold actions are refined into sustainable, strategic change. The act of aiming does not occur before movement begins; it takes place while in motion, guided by reflection and responsiveness. This is where discernment matures and where intentions become finely honed.

The "aim" step honors the wisdom gained from doing. It acknowledges that no plan is perfect from the outset, but that through real-world feedback and courageous adjustment, a good plan can become a great one. Leaders must be committed not only to acting but also to learning from that action. They must ask: What is working? What is not? What do we now see that we could not have seen before we began?

Mid-course corrections, as the "aim" in this model, are not signs of failure but of strength. They reflect deep engagement with mission, data, and discernment. Leaders who embrace the discipline of continuously ajdusting their aim understand that direction is often clarified by the journey itself.

The Courage to Let Go: Practicing Strategic Elimination

A critical, and often overlooked, component of agile leadership is the courage to admit when something isn't working. In theological education, programs and initiatives are often treated as sacrosanct. Once launched, they acquire institutional inertia, protected by tradition, ego, or fear of failure.

Effective administrators must reject the notion of "eternal security" for institutional ideas. Strategic elimination involves intentionally discontinuing programs, projects, or positions that are no longer effective or no longer aligned with the institution's mission. It means regularly asking, "Is this still serving our core purpose?"

To practice strategic elimination effectively, institutions must be mercilessly mission-driven. Every program, structure, and established pattern must be continually evaluated for its alignment with and contribution to the core mission. Sentimentality, tradition, or sunk costs must never outweigh a commitment to mission effectiveness.

One powerful evaluative tool is a simple question: If we weren't already doing this, would we start doing it now? If the answer is no, then the institution should stop engaging in that program or practice. This test cuts through legacy bias and forces leaders to view each initiative through the lens of present relevance and future potential, not past investment.

Strategic elimination is not an act of institutional coldness; it is an act of stewardship and corporate repentance. It reallocates energy and resources toward what matters most. When leaders are willing to let go of what no longer serves the mission, they create space for innovation, growth, and greater impact. Institutions that continually ask, "Is this worth starting today?" are better equipped to remain faithful, focused, and fruitful. *If your institution has never had to admit failure and strategically eliminate a project or practice, you have probably been acting too slow.*

No one bats a thousand. If you are not striking out from time to time, you aren't swinging the bat enough. You're settling for the occasional walk but letting all the home run pitches go to the catcher. *If you are not faced with the need to practice strategic elimination from time to time, you are pretending to bat a thousand... but you are not really batting a thousand.* Said another way, if your school isn't failing in small ways from time to time, it is almost certainly failing in big ways all the time.

If you are new to an institution and you want to be ready popular with your faculty and staff, walk into your first meeting and ask two questions: First, ask: "please explain what you do around here?" And then in a second round of questioning, ask: "what do you think we should quit doing?" This approach will get you much further with the faculty and staff than walking into your first meeting with a list of "new things" that an already overworked faculty and staff have to add to their workload.

Cultivating a "Ready, Fire, Aim" Culture

Creating this kind of cultural shift requires more than inspiring language; it demands systemic and strategic changes at every level of the institution. Here are some practical strategies for cultivating a "Ready, Fire, Aim" culture:

1. Redesign Information Gathering Processes: Gather only enough evidence — and counterevidence — to justify or falsify a course of action. As soon as action is justified (i.e., you are ready), act (i.e., fire), then be ready to adjust (i.e., aim). Remember the pandemic: Change can occur quickly if motivation is sufficient. Teach everyone to be comfortable acting on incomplete knowledge.

2. Normalize Pilot Projects and Provisional Launches: Institutions should frequently use language like "trial run," "pilot program," or "phase one" to lower the stakes of innovation. This reframing allows for faster initiation and more honest evaluation. A pilot culture conveys permission to try, learn, and revise. Teach everyone to expect mid-course corrections and strategic eliminations. Publicly reward informative failures as the rich learning experience that they are.

3. *Create Feedback Loops That Encourage Iteration:* Leaders should establish structured moments of reflection after implementation. This could take the form of debrief sessions, learning reviews, or check-in milestones. Faculty and staff should know that their observations will be acted upon and that revisions are part of the process, not signs of failure. Teach everyone to be willing to adapt—even to admit failure.

4. *Align Performance Metrics with Adaptability:* Institutions must assess teams not only by outcomes but by responsiveness and learning. Recognizing adaptability and initiative in annual evaluations, promotions, and public recognition reinforces the value of agility. Teach everyone that you don't expect them to bat a thousand.

5. *Lead by Example:* Administrators must be transparent about their own decision-making processes. Sharing stories of risk, adjustment, and growth demonstrates that even top leaders are committed to learning through action. When leaders model flexibility and courage, it signals that these values are not only permitted but expected. Inform everyone about your mid-course corrections and strategic eliminations. Kill off dead end projects publicly rather than allowing them to die a quiet death. By doing so, you will normalize strategic eliminations.

6. *Provide Psychological Safety:* Perhaps most importantly, cultivating this culture requires creating an environment where people feel safe to fail, reflect, and try again. Faculty and staff must trust that experimentation will be supported and that mid-course corrections will be treated as strengths, not shortcomings. Show everyone that courage is rewarded.

7. Spread the credit and hoard the blame: Some ideas will work; some will not. Own very failed idea; embrace every unsuccessful project; and claim every misstep as your own. Heap praise on everyone who was even remotely involved with a successful idea or project.

By institutionalizing these practices, seminaries can build cultures that are dynamic rather than defensive, bold rather than brittle. In such cultures, innovation becomes habitual, and responsiveness to the Spirit and to the needs of the world becomes a shared institutional posture.

Conclusion: The High Stakes of Hesitation
Academic administrators face tremendous pressures. The temptation to delay decisions until absolute certainty can be overwhelming. But in a landscape shaped by uncertainty and change, hesitation can be more dangerous than error.

Administrators must learn to recognize when they are ready—not perfectly ready, but ready enough. They must then have the courage to fire, and the wisdom to aim as they go forward with mid-course corrections and strategic eliminations. They must not fear failure but embrace learning. They must prune to grow. And they must trust that leadership, like discipleship, is an ongoing journey of faith, courage, and constant recalibration.

"Ready, Fire, Aim" is not a reckless strategy. It is a model of bold, adaptive, mission-driven leadership for the future of theological education.

Thomas E. Phillips (Ph.D., M.Div., MLS, MA) is the executive director of the Digital Theological Library. Before assuming that role, he was a professor of New Testament for nearly 20 years.

The Digital Theological Library (www.thedtl.org) is a nonprofit corporation co-owned by more than 100 seminaries. Its mission is to help everyone to engage in self-critical reflection upon their own faith and in humble dialogue with those of other traditions. The DTL fulfills this mission through the curation of digital library resources for its member institutions, religious professionals and interested individuals. The DTL also fulfills this mission through publishing religious studies content.

Practicing Innovation
Fostering Fresh Expressions of Theological Education

Greg Henson
Shanda Stricherz

Over the past fifteen years, I have had the opportunity to work with hundreds of Christian organizations ranging from Bible colleges, seminaries, and universities, to local churches, denominations, mission agencies, and faith-based nonprofits. My conversations with the leaders of those organizations have taken me down dirt roads in Africa, across sand dunes near the Persian Gulf, into countless conference rooms, and onto video production sets. Between the sunburn, stale coffee, and Zoom fatigue, the conversations routinely turned, in some way, to the question, "What is the future of theological education?"

This makes sense because administrators in theological schools face a familiar tension. The pressures of enrollment, finance, accreditation, and reputation often demand visible results, while the mission of forming people for participation in God's work demands patience, discernment, and integrity. In recent years the language of innovation has become the bridge we hope will carry us across that tension. Yet innovation in practice often settles into tactical adjustments to programs, marketing, or delivery, while the deeper realities that shape institutional life remain untouched. The result is busy activity that rarely changes the conditions that produce the outcomes we wish to improve. It seems that our approaches to innovation or change may not be having the desired impact? Might it be time to live into a renewed approach to innovation?

This essay proposes a framework for innovation that begins with theological commitments and moves through organizational life to concrete practices. While staying rooted in the kingdom of God, it calls for a renewed approach that confronts barriers directly and cultivates embodied practices so that fresh expressions of theological education can emerge and endure.

Why Innovate?

I suggest there are three primary reasons we need to invest significant time, energy, and resources into the work of innovation.

(1) Because it is an act of stewardship (Matthew 25:19-21)

We participate in the work of innovation because we are stewarding vast storehouses full of God's resources (i.e., ten talents). We must not strive merely for sustainability or survival. Faithful stewards are productive conduits (as opposed to protective managers) of God's blessing. This requires ongoing attentiveness to the way God's resources are being utilized and the fruit we are seeing, thereby encouraging ongoing change.

(2) Because we are sent by Jesus into the world (John 20:21)

We participate in the work of innovation because we have been sent by Jesus to participate in God's grand renewal project by the power of the Spirit. We cannot rest in our places of comfort and power. Instead, we practice the way of Jesus as we participate in the creativity of God – welcoming the change it requires of us.

(3) Because practicing the way of Jesus requires ongoing discernment (John 16:13)

We participate in the work of innovation because practicing the way of Jesus is a formational, long-term, ever-unfolding, developmentally-oriented endeavor that requires ongoing communal discernment. That is to say this work requires continual change.

Fortunately, most people tend to agree that we are called to participate in God's kingdom mission and to be faithful stewards of the finances, opportunities, capital and people God places in our care. That begs the question, "If we are theologically committed to being faithful stewards and have invested so much time and energy in innovation, why do our efforts often fall flat?" Perhaps it is because in our journeys of change, we find obstacles that impede our progress. These barriers to innovation often cause us to settle for technical change rather than forge ahead into the frontier of innovation.

Barriers to Innovation in Theological Education

The barriers to innovation seem to settle into five areas. They are:

Competitive Governance Structures

Governance within institutions tends to be a competition for power, resources, influence, time, energy, and attention. In our attempts to divvy up the work of an institution, we set the stage for people to put on blinders, focus on one particular aspect of the work, and then become champions for that one cause. In reality, such division of effort often fosters distrust, dis-integration, and silos, as well as battles over finances, control, and decision-making. Shared governance often creates a divisive rather than collaborative culture. One that births conflicting views of reality.

Conflicting Views of Reality

The internal competition for power and resources created by our default approach to shared governance creates fertile ground for conflicting narratives. Each narrative describes a problem to be solved (i.e., a reality) and every solution privileges the narrative from which it was birthed. Without a shared understanding of reality, we cannot have a shared problem to solve. Without a shared problem to solve innovation efforts will be scattered at best and detrimental at worst. When innovation efforts are scattered, we tend to assume we need more money to invest in more innovation.

Resource-Dependent Mindsets

When we enter the space of innovation under the impression that we need more of something, it results in an unhelpful, perhaps even deforming, resource-dependent mindset. God has entrusted us with all of the resources we need to do the tasks God has laid before us. So, if we believe our general approach is correct and we simply need to do a better job when it comes to program development, marketing, etc., then we begin to think that whatever "innovative" thing we want to do will require additional resources. We need to keep the machine running (so the thinking goes), which means the time and energy we have to invest in an alternative future is wrapped up in a search for additional resources. This resource-dependent mindset also keeps us from examining our deeper institution-shaping ideas and structures, especially the educational philosophy that is often taken for granted.

Unexamined Educational Philosophies

Our innovation efforts are stunted by the fact that we rarely envision our educational philosophy to be part of the problem. By avoiding an examination of this philosophy, we open the door to a never-ending blame game wherein we continually point at other things as "the" problem. The educational philosophy that animates the work within the institutions we serve, especially when those institutions operate within the context of higher education, impacts every aspect of our work and must be examined.

Creative Paralysis

The best way to be innovative is to do something, learn from it, and then make adjustments. Unfortunately, we tend to think that innovation is fundamentally about creating ideas. This kind of focus is the enemy of execution. It paralyzes our ability to move forward in an iterative and ongoing fashion.

Practicing Innovation

What, then, do we do to overcome these barriers and foster fresh expressions of theological education? In my experience, there are eight practices that can be grouped into three areas of focus. Taken together, these practices provide a structure for discerning, developing, implementing, and evaluating the work of innovation by helping to shape communal participation in the ongoing mission of God.

Trustworthy Community

For innovation to take root in the context of a seminary, we must create community (e.g., a shared sense of belonging) that is trustworthy (e.g., exhibits characteristics that encourage loyalty). Such community comes when we align our values and practices, solve problems together in love, and be transparent even when it is hard.

Practice #1: Practice What You Preach: Aligning espoused values and lived experience

In most cases our espoused values tend to compete with those of modern academic and hierarchical structures. Unfortunately, our practice may not be aligned with those espoused values. To combat the misalignment, we must engage in practices that require an ever-deepening embodiment of espoused institutional values in service of mission.

We engage in this practice by empowering all voices in our community. That requires fostering transparent conversations that name our values, defining our values in practical terms, and identifying areas of misalignment. In practice that means lofty words like "justice" must be described in real-life terms using real-life examples (i.e., we can't preach justice and put students in debt at the same time). Finally, we must continually address this misalignment, which cultivates a posture of learning. In doing so, we nurture new processes for empowering and listening to all voices in the community. This will be disruptive because the traditional processes for including voices will become antiquated and harmful.

Practice #2: Risk Openness: Stewarding resources with transparency

To foster fresh expressions of theological education we need to embrace "radical" transparency. It's only radical in the sense that it is very different from what we currently do. All I mean is sharing the same quantitative data with the staff, board, and faculty of an institution. Audited financial statements, donation reports, student enrollment numbers, monthly financial statements, debt and endowment figures, etc. should be available to everyone, all in the same format.

We can't stop at quantitative data, however, because it is one side of the resource story. We also need to be transparent with information about the work of the school, the opportunities in front of us, and the allocation of our time and energy. The best way I have seen this done is to create a regular and consistent "reporting" mechanism that shares information with everyone, again in the same format. By being transparent with data, we not only help the school align its values and lived experience but also build loyalty.

Practice #3: Practice Trust: Developing a resilient community

While shared meals, time together, and collaboration can be helpful avenues for building trust within a community, data from the National Survey on Brand and Trust shows that trust is built or lost through competence, problem solving, and concern for others. Each of those must be addressed through the lens of people and policies.

By fostering conversations which focus on alignment and doing so with transparency, we bring to light our concern for others, demonstrate competence, and solve problems together as a community. In this process we demonstrate care for those within the organization and commitment to the mission and kingdom calling of the organization itself. This cultivates the trust required for a web of trusting relationships to be present within a community. When we have resiliency, ongoing and transformational innovation become possible because we begin to trust that insights, wisdom, and innovation can come from anywhere in the organization. No longer must programs be developed solely by faculty or strategic wisdom come only from the board. Trustworthy community welcomes, even encourages, distributed wisdom.

Shared Reality

Our hopes for fostering fresh expressions of theological education will be dashed if we fail to develop a shared reality. Because one's view of reality shapes understanding of the problem, it dictates the solutions that may be offered. The following two practices leverage the preceding three by connecting values, information, people, and policies to the work of problem identification and strategy development.

Practice #4: Define reality: Rallying around the problem you are trying to solve

The best way to define reality is to humanize it. Defining reality requires us to be radically transparent, to say hard things about numbers, and to bring to light that our educational philosophy may very well be the problem (e.g., credit hours are a social construction that privilege certain classes of people and have no bearing on learning or reality). More importantly, it requires us to listen attentively to the people who have avoided us and to those who have seen the underbelly of the institution's history. When our conversations stay focused on numbers, budgets, programs, and the like, it is easy for us to miss the tangible impact of our words, opinions, and decisions.

Practice #5: Listen to the Spirit: Clarifying direction while welcoming diversity

The danger with defining reality is that once we do it, we tend to let that frame be the one we use for many years to come. We then develop a plan for addressing the challenges within that box and subsequently launch our new initiatives. I refer to this as taking a bounded set approach to strategy.

Instead, our strategic work needs to focus on discerning and identifying the direction in which we are being led by the Spirit. Doing so helps us define reality in terms of direction rather than specific programs, staffing models, organizational structures, and numerical goals. As a result, our shared view of reality remains open to ongoing reflection, discernment, and refinement. It can be continually shaped by our conversations about alignment, the data regarding the resources God is entrusting us with, and opportunities the Spirit is placing in front of us. This will require us to dismantle the approach we take to conversations about strategy (to become more real-time and iterative) and reconsider the artifact those conversations produce (so that it points in a direction rather than specifying a plan).

Empowering Structures

Our governance structures, organizational design, and change management processes all have the power to fuel or snuff out innovation. Even if we are successful in building a trustworthy community and a shared understanding of reality, our work will come to a grinding halt if we fail to implement empowering structures. As long as our work is bound up in structures which either push against innovation or assume innovation is primarily a task of generating and implementing new ideas in the form of new programs or educational offerings, we will not see meaningful fruit.

Practice #6: Release power: Empowering new voices through collaborative governance

The internal competition for resources, time, energy, and attention is a natural byproduct of shared governance structures that are rooted in a "divide-and-conquer" approach to organizational development. It is also natural for such structures to privilege certain voices thereby imbuing those voices with extraordinary power. For innovation to take root within our organizations, that power must be released and distributed. Power for curricular control must be distributed among staff, administrators, external partners, and students. Power for strategy development, financial oversight, and institutional identity of the wider community must be distributed in the same fashion.

Practice #7: Think Broadly: Configuring ecosystems

Anything we do in the life of an institution engaged in theological education impacts everything we do in that same institution. Therefore, whatever fresh expressions we hope to launch must account for this interconnected and interdependent reality of institutional life. I refer to this as "integrated innovation" and requires organizations to consider multiple aspects of their work at once rather than focusing energy on trying to build a better "product."

Practice #8: Adapt freely: Celebrating failure and resisting permanence

Building on the practice of following the Spirit, adapting freely requires following the same process of listening, analyzing, adapting, implementing and listening again. We add in the opportunity to celebrate "failure" and drive home the fact that developing something "permanent" is not our goal. We are simply developing the next iteration. Warner Burke perhaps said it best when he noted, "the change initiative must never stop." This should resonate with us because we too, as the people of God, are continually being remade by the work of the Spirit.

Moving Forward

Fostering fresh expressions of theological education is perhaps the most important work we can be doing as theological educators. In the United States, the last four decades have seen exorbitant rises in tuition, student debt, and dropout rates coupled with a rise and then dramatic fall in enrollment, precipitous declines in the perceived value of theological education, and a growing chasm between the local church and the academy. Ted Smith refers to this as an unraveling (which is a better and more accurate narrative than decline).

During that time, we have invested significant amounts of time, energy, and financial resources into what has been called innovation. It seems that we may need to look on this challenge with fresh eyes. Doing so requires a willingness to engage in practices that help us overcome the barriers that have impeded our progress thus far. In doing so, we will be empowered to join in the creative reality of the Kingdom by following Jesus on mission as we steward followers of Jesus who flourish in their vocations.

Greg Henson is the President and Chief Executive Officer of Kairos University and a Professor of Leadership and Organizational Formation. He holds a Doctor of Ministry from Sioux Falls Seminary and an MBA from Benedictine University, with earlier undergraduate credentials from William Jewell College. During his tenure, his work in innovation, theological education, organizational transformation, and governance has been applied across seminaries, universities, churches, and nonprofits on six continents. Previously, he also served in pastoral ministry and has long emphasized practical theology, collaborative systems, and fresh expressions of theological education.

Shanda Stricherz is Executive Vice President and Chief Creative Officer at Kairos University. She has nearly 25 years of experience in the field of theological education. Among her areas of expertise are strategic planning, institutional effectiveness, accreditation, high-level project management, communications, and student services. She is one of the key leaders in the transformation that happened at Kairos University through the Kairos Project.

Kairos University serves as a hub for a global network of partner schools and operates on a competency-based theological education (CBTE) model. It is accredited by the Higher Learning Commission and by the Commission on Accrediting of the Association of Theological Schools and offers a full spectrum of degree offerings from certificates through doctoral level, including associate degrees, bachelor's degrees, Master of Arts, Master of Divinity, Master of Arts, Doctor of Ministry, Doctor of Professional Counseling, Doctor of Theology, and Doctor of Philosophy.

Widening Access in Higher Education, Opportunities and Challenges for Students with Complex Needs

Ian Birch[1]

The Scottish Baptist College is situated in, and validated by, the University of the West of Scotland, an institution that prides itself on being number one among HE institutions in Scotland for widening access for students from disadvantaged backgrounds.[2] As a Christian theological college, we fully share this commitment to students, who, in their teens, missed the usual pathways into higher education, being given another chance later in life to fulfil their potential and pursue their vocational goals by studying for a degree in their chosen field. The Scottish Baptist College, like our host university is an institution of opportunity. Now, while we take some pride in being open

---

[1] Written in collaboration with Rev. Charles Maasz, CEO Glasgow City Mission, and governor/trustee of the Scottish Baptist College.

[2] For the policy on 'Widening Access' in Scottish Universities see "Report on Widening Access 2022-23, *Scottish Funding Council* https://web.archive.org/web/20250000000000*/https://www.sfc.ac.uk/publications/report-on-widening-access-2022-23/#top). The policy of social inclusion in HE at UWS is embedded in the 2030 Strategy Document: "Maximising our students' success," University of the West of Scotland https://web.archive.org/web/20250000000000*/https://www.uws.ac.uk/strategy2030/our-goals/maximising-our-students-success/.

for students to study theology who thought there was no way, this policy brings challenges and frustrations because we attract students with flawed and dysfunctional backgrounds, that is, students with complex needs (from now on: SWCN). This is the theme I want to reflect on in this essay.

To make my topic clear, I am thinking about "Stuart"[1] who had a background in drug addiction as a teenager and after becoming a Christian in his twenties felt called to a ministry reaching other addicts and so applied to join our BD programme. Stuart threw himself into the course but found studying to be hard going, and I soon came to realise that addiction leaves a terrible legacy of cognitive impairment making it difficult to concentrate for even short periods of time, weakened memory, struggles with comprehension, but he did not quit. At the end of the first year Stuart got his results and with one resit required would pass the course, upon which news he withdrew from the programme and moved to the Scottish Highlands to find work. No effort of persuasion on our part could reverse his decision to leave the course, and though at the time I didn't understand all that was going on, I had the sense that his first taste of success had overwhelmed him and that it was more than he could process and cope with emotionally.

I recall "Janie" who left school at 16 under pressure to help with the family income, despite having the desire and potential to take her education further. What followed was a dysfunctional marriage which included alcohol abuse, and eventually a breakdown of the relationship. In her early forties, Julie found faith in Jesus through the love and support of a friend, and after remarrying was

---

[1] The names have been changed in the essay, but the example stories are authentic.

encouraged by her new husband to fulfil her dreams of going to university. She signed up to study theology to enable her to reflect on her own journey of faith and provide a foundation for her new vocation in social services, specialising in addiction. All appeared to be going well as she completed the week-to-week tasks set for class preparation, she engaged in class conversation and was not showing outward signs of stress.

Problems first manifested when she refused to submit the first assignment for marking, and on asking about this I got the answer that she knew it wasn't "good enough." With a little persuasion she eventually submitted her work, and though the quality wasn't high there was enough content to be given a pass grade. Hoping this would boost Janie's confidence, I met to talk over the assessment process with her only to be greeted with a letter of withdrawal. Puzzled as to why she was taking this decision, she explained she couldn't believe she had passed the assessment on her own merit and was sure we were just being kind in assigning the mark, she felt that she didn't belong at university, and the pressure in her mind was about to explode. No amount of offers of support and reassurance about the external approval of her marks could persuade her to receive the affirmation of her ability, and with a word of thanks for our trying to help her, she was gone, and we were left bewildered, frustrated and profoundly sad. It was a case of "snatching defeat from the jaws of victory," what psychologists call "defence of the psyche."[1]

---

[1] See Donald Kalsched, "Revisioning Fordham's 'Defences of the Self' in Light of Modern Relational Theory and Contemporary Neuroscience," *The Journal of Analytical Psychology* 60.4 (2015): 477-80.

I could go on multiplying the stories of students in similar circumstances, some from better, some from worse situations of dysfunction and brokenness in their former life, and all with this in common: they wanted to use education as a means of amplifying the transformation faith in Jesus had brought to their lives and fulfilling their sense of unrealised potential, and then at the moment when success was with their grasp, they rejected the opportunity to score a win in life.

Our experience here in Scotland has been that too often SWCN have failed to complete the course they embarked upon, usually, though not always, not able to complete one year of the programme. Could they not do the work, you may ask? Yes, they were capable of the work. Did teachers not support them and guide them? Yes, teachers and the chaplain invested a great deal of time in pastoral and academic support for each one. The reasons why SWCN regularly do not complete their course are more complex than any one explanation can provide, but recent investigation has brought to light important insights into the issue.

Euphoria

It is commonly observed that converts to Christian faith from highly dysfunctional backgrounds exhibit a sense of euphoria, or hyperarousal, feelings of release and freedom from the bondage of addiction and/or abuse, and/or chaotic lifestyle. What follows from this is an acute appetite for the good things that life has to offer, a desire to make amends for wasted time and poor choices, wanting to "restore the years the locusts have eaten" (Joel 2:25). With a rush of courage and enthusiasm they want to break into HE to become what they know they can be and accomplish what they know they can achieve. What can possibly go wrong?

Once into the HE system, SWCN can have a light-switch experience in which euphoria flips over to feeling overwhelmed by the expansive horizon that has opened before them. Suddenly, hope and anticipation for the future is replaced by doubt, fear, insecurity, unworthiness, imposter syndrome, terror. "Inner demons" gnaw their confidence and torment their sense of identity on the inside, and around them nay-sayers, critics, envious friends and family remind them of who they really are and where they came from.

Not initially, but in time, as the course progresses, the outcome for SWCN is disturbingly familiar, which is self-sabotage. As in Janie's case, students will settle into the routine of study and give the appearance of coping, even enjoying the work that is given, but gradually it becomes noticeable that they are engaging in class less, avoiding participation unless the conversation can be steered to what is familiar. Instead of theology providing answers to the deep and complex questions they have been nursing, and a foundation for a secure life, the discursive style of learning is received as deconstructing, critical, disorienting, unsettling, where certainties are a scarce commodity and only opinions, perspectives and points of view are on offer. Add to this, the SWCN may be sitting in a classroom alongside able students who take critical thinking and oxymorons in their intellectual stride, and so, the big talk, the exuberance, the enthusiasm for this new life, the new "me," does not last. What seeps into the mind are high levels of stress, anxiety, worries about finances and anticipations of failure, lack of self-esteem, survivor guilt, all of which become triggers for failure, and drop-out inevitably follows.[1]

The medical world tells us that what has happened is something like an auto-immune disease of the psyche, primitive defences in the realm of the psyche caused by previous trauma. The defence mechanisms developed as a means of survival in the face of unbearable input from the environment, "protecting something absolutely essential in the personality that must never be violated."[2] In a complex process of psychological paradox, when life improves and genuine opportunity for self-activation and aliveness presents itself, as is happening for SWCN, the inner defence system makes an inaccurate evaluation of the situation and sees this as a dangerous invitation to the old disasters of hopes dashed and expectations shattered and attacks them accordingly.[3] The capacity for self-attacking and self-destructive energies in SWCN is great and disturbing to teachers trying to guide them to a state of acceptance with their successes.

Speaking with SWCN at the point they resign from the course, or simply stop attending classes, it usually emerges that the positive student experience has been eroding for considerable time, and the decision to quit, though seemingly sudden, was the inevitable step in an evolving process. The quantity and level of reading, the research and preparation for each class, gradually had become overwhelming. The effort to keep up with others in the class was exhausting, the discipline required to think hard and deep, and to persist with work when physically

---

[1] Psychologists call this "shut-down." See Bessel van der Kolk, *The Body Keeps the Score* (London: Penguin, 2014), 99.
[2] Kalsched, "Defences of the self," 480.
[3] Van der Kolk, *The Body Keeps the Score*, 74.

and mentally tired, became just too much. But who knew? Each week the body was there in class, the eyes seemed bright, the student appeared to be engaged, but in reality they were wrestling with a process of denial, telling themselves they could do it and suppressing the burgeoning sense of hopelessness, avoidance of the inner conflict, eventually becoming numb to the psychological dissonance, though eventually all of this bursts out into the open, and exit becomes the only, and to them, absolutely necessary, means of survival.

So what is to be done, is there any way of helping SWCN to survive the course, overcome the barriers to success, achieve the transformation that education can offer? For sure, there is no recipe for certain or guaranteed success, but there are ways to support SWCN better, which has the benefit of giving teachers slightly more confidence that we did all we could to help these students, regardless of their identities or backgrounds, achieve their goals.

What can be done?

I want to mention eight practical ways which might be useful to hold in mind when welcoming a SWCN onto a new course at university. This is not a method, more a random list of behaviours the teacher might adopt according to the circumstances.

1. Do not over empathise with a SWCN. It is common for a SWCN to perceive that the teacher is hiding their real self behind their professional role, a sad, but real part, of the delusional world and self-perception of a SWCN. When the teacher makes an extra effort to be attentive, affirming, encouraging, praising, it backfires because it reinforces the student's perception that no one is being honest with them. They "know" they are inadequate,

unworthy, out of their depth, why is everyone pretending otherwise?
2. Do not lower the boundaries and expectations of what is required of a SWCN, as this gives wiggle room for exploitation of the teacher and the system. Lowering expectations and being lenient reinforces to a SWCN that they are not really good enough for the class, and they are being treated differently, they are a "special case." Critical feedback for a weak performance in class or assessments is an important instance of the good-and-bad that must be held together as an expression of truth and reality which is part of life.
3. Expect that a SWCN will have to work harder than most other students toward their successes, but success must be their success, not gained on account of compassion. It can be helpful to have a third party, a support worker, check in regularly with the student to encourage them to keep going, and assist with class tasks.
4. Be real and authentic with SWCN, as they, of all students, recognise patronising sympathy when not entirely genuine. The deeper purpose of this approach, beyond the mere question of integrity, is that SWCN will realise they are in a safe space to express their challenges and receive critique and correction.
5. Studies have shown that having a support network, or at least one person who generates a sense of safety is crucial for enabling a SWCN to navigate the new world of HE.[1] A SWCN will benefit significantly from the appointment of a mentor or advocate who

---

[1] See Van der Kolk, *The Body Keeps the Score*, 251.

they meet at the beginning of the course and someone who will check in regularly with them, especially during the first week of their student journey. At our institution the person perfectly positioned for this role is the college chaplain, who teaches on the course, but takes a position aloof from the staff to be a "safe" person for students to reach out to, knowing their conversation is confidential and without limits.

6. It is important for staff to recognise the emotional stage/age a student is at when they join a course, as this may be the same as the yearly age at which they engaged in addictive habits.

7. Remember that SWCN are on a personal journey, which is true for all students who enter a university course, but their starting point is probably a great deal further back than most others. I have encountered SWCN who do not lack native intelligence but have had very little exposure to books, have written very little, and read texts rarely. Many are the first in their family to ever attend university and lack any cultural context for the step they are taking into the world of HE.

8. Work at cultivating resilience in SWCN. The partnership between a teacher and SWCN is vital if there is to be a hope of success with the students, the relationship providing security in which the student can be nurtured into processing the setbacks and receiving the successes. Van Der Kolk suggests techniques such as yoga and mindfulness can also help in this process of developing resilience, but these are not usually within the scope of a teacher to provide, though at the Scottish Baptist College we are fortunate to work within a university that

provides excellent student support via professional educational counsellors, and students are encouraged to access this help.

Lisa Miller's work in the field of psychology has demonstrated the link between spirituality and resilience and has demonstrated that altruism and relational spirituality can aid the development of the existential core of a person.[1] This suggests to me that instead of the teacher focussing excessively on the learning experience of a SWCN, which we are tempted to do, the student might be invited to work with another student, a peer group member, giving the SWCN a focus away from themselves and an opportunity to invest in someone, and something, external to their own needs. Van der Kolk speaks of resilience as "the product of agency: knowing that what you do can make a difference,"[2] which implies the same thing, and points in the same direction.

Conclusion

It is our intention and purpose at the Scottish Baptist College to eschew all forms of elitism, while remaining committed to high standards of academic work in the HE sector. We endeavour to make a pathway into theological education and vocational training for anyone who feels called to walk this path, while we are not so naive to think anyone can complete a degree in theology and some are best served enrolling into a lighter programme. The issue with SWCN is not whether they are clever enough to undertake the course, that question will have been established prior to them starting, but whether a dysfunctional, addictive or

---

[1] Lisa Miller, *The Awakened Brain* (Dublin: Allen Lane, 2021), 41-2 & 222-3

[2] Van der Kolk, *The Body Keeps the Score*, 426-27.

abusive background will subvert what they might achieve if it is not for the self-destructive power at work in their spirit/psychology. We cannot guarantee all who begin their degree will complete the course and graduate with honours, but those who do so are utterly transformed by the experience, and receive the public validation of their achievement, and their worth to society, as redemption of their utmost being. This is the value of education, and if we can do better and enable SWCN to achieve more then let us learn from one another, and pass on what we learn, in order to be more effective in the goals we have set ourselves.

Scottish Baptist College (SBC), located in Scotland, is a theological institution committed to delivering accessible, degree-level theological education rooted in Baptist traditions yet open to diverse Christian convictions. It offers a flexible range of modes—full-time, part-time, and modular study—allowing students to complete programmes from one-year certificates to a four-year Bachelor of Divinity (Honours) in Theology with Pastoral Studies. SBC values a learning community composed of students from varied life stages and backgrounds, aiming to equip learners to engage in Christian faith and mission in both church and public life.

Rev. Dr. Ian Birch is Principal of Scottish Baptist College, where he also teaches biblical studies, ethics, church history, Christian leadership, and Baptist identity and heritage. Born on the Wirral in Cheshire, he spent about twenty-five years in pastoral ministry, serving congregations in Gillingham, Southsea, St Helens, and Kirkintilloch before joining SBC as full-time staff in 2008. His academic credentials include degrees in theology (University of Wales / Spurgeon's College), biblical studies (Open University / ICC), and a PhD in historical theology from the University of St Andrews. Recognized for teaching excellence, he holds the status of Principal Fellow of the Higher Education Authority (PFHEA). Under his leadership, SBC emphasizes rigorous scholarship rooted in Baptist convictions, equipping students for both academic and ministry vocations.

Trinity Leadership Fellows
Sharing God's Love through Service to Communities

Robert Garris

The title of this volume, with its focus on service, speaks directly to my understanding of theological education and leadership development, the field of education I have worked in for years. Since my earliest years as a teenager in the Episcopal Church I have understood the gospel as a call to serve our fellow humanity in spiritual or physical need. And throughout the decades that I've worked in graduate level education in public policy and leadership development, that commitment to serve others in need again informed how I understand leadership development. At Trinity Church in New York City, I have had the privilege of weaving together my faith and my experience in leadership development, in the creation of the Trinity Leadership Fellows program.

In building a leadership program focused on service to those in need, we did not adopt a singular focus on the well-developed servant leadership literature but instead operate with a lens that sees all types of leadership, including the ministry of faith leaders, as anchored in serving those in need and empowering them to lead in their own right. This is the primary focus of the selection process for our fellows program. The entire educational experience is infused with the shared sense of purpose and commitment to service among our fellows. They are learning via our curriculum and supporting each other in their journeys, strengthening their capacity to serve their congregations and communities and to advance the Kingdom of God in everyday tangible ways in their neighborhoods.

The curriculum shares much in common with programs offered by some of the world's leading business and non-profit management programs, with two distinctive differentiators: faith and community. Faith infuses the entire curriculum and experience. Throughout, fellows are asked to articulate confidently and consistently how the values that are embedded in their faith shape the challenging decisions they will have to make as leaders.

And across the entire curriculum, fellows are challenged to build up their skills in sustaining relationships, with each other, with their congregations, with their communities. Across classes, they are exhorted to do things with, not for, others, thus developing the interpersonal skills needed to serve effectively. Literally every course in the curriculum is a variation on the theme of establishing, nurturing, and expanding relationships, with the goal of building God's kingdom of service to others. The curriculum also complements and strengthens the faith education efforts of other theological programs. By offering complementary coursework for emerging and advanced professionals and for supporting groups and networks who wish to learn in community, the Trinity Leadership fellows program adds to the rich offerings available to those who feel called to lead through their faith.

Building community

This education and formation program, weaving faith together with service, assumes that effective skills at building relationships and community are essential to serving and addressing physical and spiritual needs and creating positive change in the neighborhoods around us.

The first week of each year of the fellowship is an intensive, in-person experience dedicated primarily to building community within the cohort. Much of the rest of the curriculum is structured around relationship with and service to communities and congregations, but it is important to start close to home and ensure strong community within the learning cohort. In a workshop called "Understanding Yourself as a Leader," the fellows go deep and personal in small groups, sharing how their faith, beliefs, values, passions, pain, and social "wiring" shape who they are as leaders. An immediate goal of these two days of deep introspection is to produce a public statement of faith, values, and leadership, a concise way of sharing with others and articulating for themselves how their faith informs the ways that they lead. But the two-day workshop also serves the critical purpose of building community, trust, and commitment among the fellows. They will support each other not only through a twelve-month curriculum (more on that soon), but they will also serve as a community of mutual accountability in completing a second year project and then throughout their ministries and careers.

After this intensive workshop, while still in New York City, the fellows begin their first course, on Community Organizing. As with all of their coursework, this course is rooted in building and sustaining relationships, and empowering people to address their own challenges. In this case, the relationships in question cross the boundaries of any single institution (church, non-profit, business, or government office) to connect an entire community in a sense of shared purpose. As in all courses, this is taught by an active person of faith who has done this work from his house of worship in and with his or her own community. Later in the week, the fellows visit the inspiring

Nehemiah Homes in East Brooklyn, a breathtakingly successful example of congregations organizing and taking power to improve the neighborhood around them.

Together these congregations have changed their neighborhood from one of the most neglected corners of New York City into an expansive, beautiful collection of thousands of units of affordable housing, almost half of them owner-occupied. The Nehemiah Homes succeeded in a particular environment and era that cannot be simply replicated in other locations. But the principles of listening, giving power to community members, and collaboration among people of faith and government to address urgent needs in their own neighborhood transfer to almost any context, making this a powerful site visit for our fellows.

The rest of the curriculum, which is also available through FaithLeadershipCampus.org in asynchronous form online, at no cost, continues in this theme of strengthening skills for relationship and community, with the goal of serving those around us in need and building God's kingdom in our neighborhoods. Courses on Conflict Transformation and Change Management prepare our fellows for maintaining and even strengthening relationships and community in times of change. Our course on Church and Non-Profit Administration, the most "nuts and bolts" course in the curriculum, highlights people and relationships as the priority in leading an organization in every one of its case studies. People and relationships are at the core of the course on Adaptive Leadership. Whether it's examining relationships and group dynamics from the "balcony or dance floor," consciously adjusting the temperature of conflict to keep progress underway while maintaining strong relationships, understanding the relationship between stakeholders is essential in every phase of this approach to adaptive leadership. Last, but not least, the fellows' course on Social Entrepreneurship is about launching a venture that's deeply and genuinely embedded in awareness of and relationship with the community that the social venture intends to serve.

Leadership skills that recognize and value the divine in our fellow congregants, neighbors, and relationships are at the heart of this program in faith and leadership. Our curriculum draws in many ways from secular programs in non-profit and business management, but at the same time centers faith, love, relationship, and community as the foundations of faithful and effective service with and for others. By centering faith and community while building up practical leadership skills, it is our goal to create cohorts of faithful and effective leaders who can advance the Kingdom of God in their neighborhoods every day and throughout the rest of their ministries.

Robert Garris has built innovative international education and professional training programs at universities and foundations for more than twenty years, working for Schwarzman Scholars (a leadership development program in China), the Rockefeller Foundation, Columbia University, and Johns Hopkins School of Advanced International Studies. He also serves on the boards of education-related companies and non-profits in the U.S. and abroad. Rob received his Ph.D. in European History from the University of North Carolina, Chapel Hill, where he specialized in immigration and urban policy. He is currently the Executive Director of the Trinity Leadership Fellows program and Managing Director of the Leadership Development initiative on the philanthropies team at Trinity Church in New York City.

Trinity Leadership Fellows program and the Leadership Development initiative on the philanthropies team at Trinity Church in New York City. These interconnected initiatives develop the leadership capacities of people of faith, empowering them to more effectively serve urgent needs in their communities and congregations.

Trustworthy Assessment and Pastoral Formation
An Introduction to Competency Based Theological Education (CBTE)

Marjolein de Blois
Greg Henson

A Shifting Landscape

Theological education is undergoing a period of significant disruption. Traditional models that once seemed immovable are now being questioned by institutions, learners, and churches alike. Enrollment is declining across many seminaries. Financial models are under strain. Denominational loyalties have weakened, and the retention rates of pastors who stay in the ministry are declining. Studies show that five years after graduating from seminaries, very large majorities of those who graduated have left the ministry to pursue other vocations.[1] At the same time, the demands of congregational life have caused many to question whether or not conventional programs are meeting the needs of pastoral formation. These external pressures are compounded by internal doubts about whether current systems of education are doing what they were originally designed to do.

---

[1] Michael Duane Kitsko, "Early Career Attrition of Seminary Graduates: Effects of Perceived Fit, Early Childhood Experiences, Financial Debt, and Mentoring," PhD Dissertation, Michigan State University, 2019.

In light of this shifting landscape, it is not enough to tweak delivery methods or update course catalogs. What is needed is a deeper examination of the educational philosophies that shape how theological education is conceived and practiced. The assumptions that underlie credit hours, types of learning environments, and the sequencing of courses have gone largely unexamined. At the same time, institutions are looking for operational models that are more sustainable and more responsive to the church. Both of these dimensions, the philosophical and the practical, need to be held together.

This essay suggests Competency Based Theological Education (CBTE) as a response to this moment. CBTE is not a new delivery method or an administrative alternative. It is a philosophy of theological education that brings theological formation, educational philosophy, and institutional practice into alignment. Drawing on the work of Kenton Anderson and Gregory Henson in *Theological Education: Principles and Practices of a Competency Based Approach*, this essay will survey the current climate, examine the prevailing assumptions that shape it, and propose CBTE as a coherent response with both theoretical and practical implications.

The Current Climate

The long history of theological education represents a journey from intimate, relational learning by following and learning directly from Jesus to increasingly systematized and institutionalized approaches of modern Western education. In the early days of the Christian movement, students followed spiritual leaders and learned through experience. It was not until the High Medieval period that intellectual attainments supplanted a more practically oriented apprenticeship model. This was later solidified in times typically labelled as the Enlightenment. Of course, this development did not unfold in a straight line, and there were always exceptions, even at the height of the university model in Western Europe and North America. Often this shift to the university model went hand in hand with the establishment position of Christian churches in particular nations and contexts. In such cases, the minister was a cultural authority figure and looked up to because of his position and theoretical knowledge. As such, theological education focused on the transmission of theory, debate with fellow students, learning from the masters, and entering communities as religious experts.

The climate has shifted. Christianity no longer holds the cultural hegemony today in most contexts, and the ministry seldom occupies the privileged cultural position that is sustained by a government or the larger cultural environment. Theological education today exists within a fragile institutional ecosystem. For many seminaries and divinity schools, the combination of rising costs and declining enrollment has placed long term sustainability in question. Schools that once served as denominational flagships now face existential uncertainty. Some have closed. Others have merged. Still others operate under increasing financial strain. We suggest these realities are not merely budgetary problems. They reflect deeper questions about the role and relevance of theological education in a rapidly changing cultural and educational landscape.

At the same time, the church is changing. Fewer learners arrive with strong denominational ties or clear pathways into ministry. Many pursue preparation in the absence of institutional support. Churches are asking whether graduates are prepared not only to think and reason theologically but to lead, shepherd, and serve in complex social and spiritual environments both within the church as well as within society. Over the past 40 years, the longstanding assumption that a Master of Divinity degree reliably leads to competent pastoral leadership has slowly and persistently been challenged from within the academy and the church.

Cultural patterns have shifted as well. Due to financial need, learners often work full time while studying. Many are already engaged in ministry and need education that supports, rather than interrupts, that work. Leaving the ministry, uprooting their families, and moving to another city for four years of seminary training is for many not an option. Others seek models that recognize prior experience and demonstrated skill. The traditional classroom-centered, time-bound approach struggles to adapt to this complexity. It was built for a different generation, serving a different kind of church, in a different cultural moment.

Taken together, these realities suggest the need for serious reexamination. Institutional instability, shifting ecclesial expectations, and changing learner demographics have created a climate in which inherited models can no longer be assumed to serve the purposes for which they were created. The challenge is not only operational. It is philosophical and theological as well. It is a challenge that not only addresses what we learn, but how we shape skilled and committed leaders who serve and keep on serving in complex and pressured times. The solution must be rooted in mission, not survivability. The goal cannot simply be for institutions to thrive lest we turn institutions into idols.

The Prevailing Educational Philosophy

Behind every educational system is a set of assumptions. In theological education, many assumptions have been inherited from the modern university. The most visible example is the credit hour. Although widely accepted and deeply embedded, the credit hour is simply a social construct. Many will agree that time is a poor measurement of learning, and some are willing to suggest alternative methods. We suggest, however, that credit hours are not only a poor measurement of learning but also a poor measurement of time. While it assumed to be a measure that standardizes instructional time, the credit hour does not even do that well. In fact, during a congressional hearing in 2010, Sylvia Manning, who was serving as president of the Higher Learning Commission at the time, noted: "The apparent precision of *the credit hour* as originally defined, based on the fact that it has numbers, *is an illusion*."[1] Nonetheless, over time it has become the primary mechanism by which learning is measured, degrees are structured, and institutional viability is monitored.

This time-based system implies a philosophy of education. It assumes that if learners spend a designated number of hours in class under the instruction of a qualified faculty member, then learning has occurred. In this way, institutions come to equate time with mastery and presence with formation. That logic tilts programs toward curriculum coverage and content delivery, often at the expense of integrated learning, contextual formation, or spiritual discernment that comes from the integrated life experiences of active ministry engagement. The unspoken assumption is that exposure to information produces learning, even when there is little evidence of demonstrated proficiency.

---

[1] *The Department of Education Inspector General's Review of Standards for Program Length in Higher Education*, 2010, p. 21, emphasis added.

Scientific models and pedagogical experts agree that learning is an integration of knowledge and practice. Cognitive learning and practical or vocational application are both essential to form a competent individual. Many churches who currently hold on to the cognitive emphasis in learning claim that it is *after* seminary training and during the first years of ministry that the graduate learns the practical skills. While churches may have practiced this approach, it has, as mentioned, led to the burnout and declining retention rates of pastors, and a wide-spread sense of ineffectiveness.

Moreover, this philosophy which emphasizes cognitive absorption tends to prioritize what can be taught and tested in traditional learning environments whether they are in-person or online. Content delivery and mastery become the center of gravity. Other dimensions of knowing are treated as secondary or as matters that develop outside the formal educational process. Structures often reinforce this separation by dividing academic departments by discipline and relegating formation to specific offices or co-curricular activities.

Scientific models and pedagogical experts agree that learning is an integration of knowledge and practice. Cognitive learning and practical or vocational application are both essential to form a competent individual. Many churches who currently hold on to the cognitive emphasis in learning claim that it is *after* seminary training and during the first years of ministry that the graduate learns the practical skills. While churches may have practiced this approach, it has, as mentioned before, led to the burnout and declining retention rates of pastors, and a wide-spread sense of ineffectiveness.

The result is an approach that struggles to serve the church and fails to embrace the integrated nature of knowing that is so deeply embedded in Scripture. Scripture never disconnects cognitive learning from character formation and life wisdom. While the current approach to learning tends to produce what Perry Glanzer refers to as "novice experts,"[1] it often fails to foster integrated knowing and formational depth because it tends to privilege abstraction over practice and content mastery over wisdom. These tendencies are not the product of negligence. They are the predictable outcomes of a system built on a particular understanding of education shaped by the embedded epistemologies of the Enlightenment. If theological education is to serve the church, it must confront not only its methods but the philosophy that underlies them. Theological education is rightly reconsidering older practices from times in which churches were culturally marginal, as is much closer to how things are today in most contexts.

The Unexamined Connection Between Philosophy and Practice

The current challenges are often framed as practical problems. Schools wrestle with enrollment, budgets, and accreditation standards. Learners want flexibility. Churches want graduates who can lead. These are treated as tactical issues. In reality, they are deeply interconnected and interdependent.

When institutions organize around the credit hour, they must build systems on fixed calendars, faculty teaching loads, and classroom-centered delivery. This

---

[1] Glanzer, Perry L. "Are You Trying to Create Experts or Mentor Students toward Excellence? The Two Are Not the Same." CHRISTIAN SCHOLAR'S REVIEW (blog), September 3, 2025.

creates structures that are difficult to adapt. The model resists innovation not simply because people resist change, but because the system is rigid by design. At the same time, these structures shape an institution's definition of success. Completion becomes the primary indicator. Degrees conferred, rather than formation, become the measurement of success. The measurement of completion does not serve the connection between church and the institution. Rather, a focus on mere academic completion may result in a student who is cognitively shaped but may be practically, spiritually, and vocationally unprepared for ministry.

Many schools were established when the path from seminary to pulpit was linear and predictable. Those who felt called to the ministry would graduate high school or college and went on to study for the ministry, even without much life or ministry experience. In a society where Christianity is the cultural norm and where there is relative cultural stability, this may have seemed to work better. The Church is in a very different place today. A model built on information transfer and time-bound instruction is neither appropriate for this time and place nor adequate for the formational endeavor of theological education in a society where the church and its values are under pressure.

In short, the institutional challenges are not only circumstantial. They reflect deeper assumptions about what it means to teach, to learn, and to form followers of Jesus who flourish in their vocations by having practiced spiritual life wisdom. If those assumptions go unchallenged, operational adjustments will be temporary at best. The future of theological education depends on bringing philosophy and practice back into alignment.

CBTE as a Response

Competency Based Theological Education, as defined and understood by its early advocates, emerges as a robust and multi-faceted response to the disconnect between the Church and the inherited structures of theological education. It recognizes that operational challenges and philosophical limitations must be addressed at the same time. Rather than starting with a list of courses or a curriculum, CBTE invites learners, institutions, and the Church to start by considering what it means to be proficient for ministry, and how that proficiency might be demonstrated. That shift is small in words and large in implications.

In contrast to time-based education, CBTE is built on the premise that learning is demonstrated through performance, not through seat time or abstract assignments. Learners advance when they demonstrate mastery of specific outcomes that arise from the needs of the church and the lived realities of ministry. In this way, CBTE restores a kind of integrity between theological education and ecclesial formation. A learner's vocational context shapes how they engage in the learning process and how they are assessed.

This model also has practical advantages. Because learning is not tied to a fixed calendar, CBTE allows for greater flexibility. Learners can move at a pace that aligns with their context. This allows learners to *stay* in their context as they learn. As such, many remain embedded in ministry, which enables real time integration of theory and practice. For institutions, this opens the possibility of new delivery models that are not constrained by classroom capacity or by structures devoted to measuring time. Rather, learning has a practical element as students minister while they learn and with the guidance of experienced trainers. The transition is not simple. Yet CBTE offers a path to address structural rigidity without sacrificing theological depth.

CBTE challenges the idea that content mastery alone is sufficient for pastoral formation. By focusing on demonstrated proficiency of integrated knowing, it calls for an educational journey that brings together content, character, skill, spiritual maturity, and contextual wisdom. It recovers an older vision of Christian formation that attends not only to biblical and theological content but to who the learner is becoming.

Trustworthy Assessment

Readers who want a fuller account of CBTE's architecture should consult *Theological Education: Principles and Practices of a Competency Based Approach by Kenton Anderson and Gregory Henson*. The book presents the core principles and institutional practices that give CBTE coherence. It is a clear and helpful starting point. Interested readers should also look to the growing set of white papers produced by Kairos University, which explore the practical details of this model and offer conceptual language that has proven helpful in implementation.

In their book, Anderson and Henson describe Holistic Assessment as a core principle of CBTE. In the years since the book was written, Kairos University, where Greg Henson serves as president, has adapted the principle of Holistic Assessment. Instead, the school has chosen to refer to Trustworthy Assessment, of which Holistic Assessment is a part. Holistic assessment remains essential. However, Trustworthy Assessment better names the comprehensive aim. It asks not only whether we are looking at the whole person, but also whether the assessment process itself can be relied upon by all stakeholders to render meaningful and fair judgments about learner readiness. To sketch the broad contours of trustworthy assessment, it helps to note both the assessment practices and the assessment characteristics that animate it in the CBTE conversation.

Trustworthy assessment involves three core practices. Faculty and mentor teams engage in attentive observation, intentional conversation, and evaluative review. While these are simple phrases, they are dense with meaning. Attentive observation emphasizes that in an outcome-based model many forms of proficiency can be observed in lived practice. Behaviors, attitudes, skills, dispositions, and cognitive abilities become visible in context, and therefore observable for the sake of guidance and growth. Intentional conversation provides space to probe and clarify what is observed. As learners articulate their thinking, ask questions, and reflect aloud, mentors can discern how learning is taking root and can offer formative feedback that guides next steps. Evaluative review attends to the artifacts learners produce as demonstrations of learning, such as projects, situational learning experiences, papers, journals, presentations, or exams, and it pairs evaluation with feedback that supports ongoing development.

These practices are animated by four characteristics that make assessment more trustworthy over time. First, assessment should be longitudinal. Evaluation is most reliable when it unfolds over a period that aligns with a learner's vocational goals, preferred pace, and program. It assumes the learner is present in a community that can observe development across time and it depends on mentor teams who are equipped to see a learner's growth from multiple angles. Second, assessment should be holistic. Trustworthy assessment insists that learners demonstrate integrated growth across domains and across dimensions of knowing. *Content, character,* and *craft* are inseparable. Weakness in one dimension can compromise the whole, so assessment must invite and evaluate integration, not simply checklists within silos.

Third, assessment should be general rather than narrowly task specific when the aim is to evaluate integrated outcomes. General rubrics create space for contextual identity and allow mentor teams to see how learners engage real problems in their communities through processes of action and reflection. By contrast, task specific rubrics can impose a single frame that may not fit context and can detach assessment from relationship. Fourth, assessment should be relational. Because God works in and through relationships, formation is inherently communal. Mentor teams journey with learners over years and therefore gain a fuller view of how the student performs and what the student needs for further learning. That trust allows for feedback that is both candid and constructive, spoken from relationship rather than positional power.

Trustworthy assessment also attends to assessment as learning, not only assessment of learning. In this approach, feedback connected to clear goals and criteria becomes a driver of growth, and learners actively use feedback to monitor progress and set next steps. The emphasis falls on metacognition and on the learner's role as an agent in formation. This orientation strengthens the reliability and the formational value of assessment at the same time. And the skills of self-reflection and adaptability through self-reflection are life skills that students will take with them throughout life and that are applicable to all dimensions of life.

In sum, trustworthy assessment reframes the conversation. It includes the holistic scope of formation, yet it presses further by asking whether the entire ecology of assessment can be trusted. It looks across time. It looks across domains and dimensions. It honors context with general rubrics that evaluate integration. It is carried within relationships that sustain honest feedback. And it cultivates a formative stance in which assessment feeds learning, not only records it.

Implications and First Steps

CBTE carries implications that reach far beyond curricular revision. At its core, CBTE invites institutions to rethink the nature of theological formation. For schools that have long operated within time-bound, faculty-centered models, this can feel disorienting. Yet the shift is not merely structural. It is theological. And it is not novel. It has been done by the church for many decades in the past. CBTE asks institutions to align their systems with the purposes they claim to serve. That is, the purpose to train comprehensively through the training of character, cognitive ability, and skillful wisdom. That kind of alignment brings both opportunity and responsibility.

The first implication is cultural. Assumptions that drive CBTE, such as formation in context, team-based mentoring, and trustworthy assessment, challenge long standing norms. Faculty remain essential, yet their engagement takes a different shape. They serve as mentors within teams and they attend to formation that is wider than academic performance. This requires humility, collaboration, and a posture that privileges accompaniment over one way transmission. But in the process of mentoring students through reflection and active engagement, also the faculty will be formed as they co-learn with the learner they guide.

Learners also experience a different journey. They are not passive recipients of content. They are active participants in formation. Because CBTE centers on demonstrated proficiency, learners must practice sustained reflection and engage in self-assessment that is anchored in vocational contexts. This can be demanding, not because it multiplies tasks, but because it asks for deeper integration. Learners are not asked simply to complete a program. They are asked to come to understand themselves with their strengths and shortcomings, to challenge themselves and be challenged in both character and knowledge, and to become trustworthy disciples of the Jesus in community, in context, and over time.

For institutions, movement toward CBTE requires changes at multiple levels. Governance structures need reconsideration. Policies designed around credit hours and classroom-based learning must be redesigned. Assessment systems must be rebuilt around trustworthy evaluation. These shifts demand serious attention, wide participation, and patient experimentation. They also require theological clarity. CBTE will not be sustained by pragmatism alone. It must be rooted in a shared sense of calling and service to the Church.

Despite the challenges, the transition is possible and already underway in diverse settings. For schools considering first steps, it is often helpful to invite others to walk with them as they get started. At the time of writing, Symporus is, in our opinion, the best such partner. They bring years of experience working with schools, churches, and denominations around the world. They can be found at Symporus.com.

If a school wishes to get started alone, the most important move is to ask foundational questions. What kind of graduates are we called to form? What kinds of learning and formation produce those outcomes? What would it look like to build a system that aligns with those answers?

From there, schools can identify or clarify their desired outcomes. These should reflect not only content, but the full range of formation, including spiritual maturity, leadership capacity, biblical literacy, theological imagination, and personal integrity. Once outcomes are defined, attention can turn to how learners will demonstrate them and how communities will assess them with trust and consistency.

Pilot programs can help. Rather than overhauling everything at once, schools can begin with a particular program, cohort, or partnership. These smaller experiments surface insights, reveal structural needs, and build momentum for broader change. Most importantly, they model what it looks like when education is shaped not by tradition alone, but by thoughtful reflection on how best to serve the church today.

Closing Remarks

Theological education is facing a moment of reckoning. Institutions are grappling with enrollment, finances, and questions of relevance. Churches are asking whether graduates are truly ready to serve and able to engage with the complex issues of life. Learners are seeking learning that is meaningful, flexible, and formational of their whole life and character. These challenges arise from assumptions about what education is and how it should function. The crisis is not solely structural or financial. It is philosophical, pedagogical, and theological.

For theological educators, the invitation is to consider CBTE begins with humility and continues through collaboration. It requires theological clarity and institutional courage. The future will not be shaped by preserving systems. It will be shaped by those willing to reimagine how formation can be faithful to the church, responsive to context, and anchored in the gospel. CBTE is one such path. It is not the only one. It is a promising one, and for many schools it may be the next faithful step.

Dr. Marjolein (Jo) de Blois has a BA in Cultural Anthropology and Development Sociology from Leiden University and an MA and PhD in New Testament Studies (Gospel of Matthew) from Puritan Reformed Theological Seminary in Grand Rapids, Michigan. She currently serves at PRTS as Chief Global Engagement Officer and leads the strategic projects of the executive team.

Puritan Reformed Theological Seminary (PRTS), located in Grand Rapids, Michigan was founded in 1995. This ATS accredited institution seeks to train students for pastoral, counseling, and teaching ministry through its range of academic programs. PRTS is known for its rigorous academic content as well as its global partnerships with seminaries serving worldwide.

Greg Henson is the President and Chief Executive Officer of Kairos University and a Professor of Leadership and Organizational Formation. He holds a Doctor of Ministry from Sioux Falls Seminary and an MBA from Benedictine University, with earlier undergraduate credentials from William Jewell College.

Kairos University is an interdenominational theological university based in Sioux Falls, South Dakota. It serves as a hub for a global network of partner schools and operates on a competency-based theological education (CBTE) model. Its mission emphasizes affordability, accessibility, and flexibility, allowing students to pursue theological formation in context through mentoring, contextual practice, and customizable learning journeys. It is accredited by the Higher Learning Commission and by the Commission on Accrediting of the Association of Theological Schools.

Part IV

On Libraries and Their Role in Theological Education

Libraries have long stood at the center of theological education. They are places of preservation, discovery, and dialogue, housing not only the texts that have shaped faith across centuries but also the tools needed to engage with emerging questions. Part IV turns our attention to the role of libraries in both sustaining and reshaping theological education.

The essays in this section highlight how libraries are more than repositories of information. They are formative spaces that help students, faculty, and communities wrestle with ideas, test assumptions, and imagine alternative futures. At a time when digital resources and new technologies are reshaping access to knowledge, libraries invite us to consider what it means to steward wisdom faithfully. They remind us that the practice of theological education is not only about creating new ideas but also about tending carefully to the traditions and conversations that precede us.

Today's Library
The Best of the Past for the Sake of the Future

Kristin Johnston Largen

In 2022, Wartburg Theological Seminary did something that, in the current climate of theological education, might seem counterintuitive, or even foolish: we began a significant remodel of our primary educational building, including our Reu Memorial Library. (And, I am pleased to say that we completed the project on time and under budget). The new space is beautiful and smaller, geared to users of today and tomorrow: among other things, we repurposed the third floor, installed compact shelving, created space for zoom collaborations, and purchased seating that better accommodates laptops.

Now, before you assume that Wartburg is stuck in the past and hopelessly out of date, you should also know that Wartburg was way ahead of the curve on digital learning. Since 2016, all degree programs are delivered using a one class, three modalities pedagogy: all classes include residential students; synchronous distance learners who zoom into the classroom using the two large TVs in the front and back of each room; and asynchronous distance learners, who are part of the learning community online. In 2020, when we had to close our campus, we kept calm and carried on with all necessary technology already in place. Additionally, Wartburg's early participation in, and support of, the Digital Theological Library has fundamentally transformed the way we think about what a library is and what a library can do.

So, in this moment, what have we learned, and where are we going? In conversation with Ericka Raber, Director of Wartburg Seminary's Reu Library, a few issues surfaced that we are going to be continuing to think about and prioritize, and I thought it would be helpful to share them here.

First, we know that ongoing issues around copyright and licensing agreements will continue to impact how [and to whom] we are able to deliver digital resources. Ericka Raber of the Reu Memorial Library notes:

> It would be great if we could make ebooks more seamlessly available to students. There are challenges that make this difficult, the biggest challenge being licensing agreements that require the use of digital rights management tools, platforms that require downloading additional software with an additional individual login to control and limit digital access. These additional tools and logins are sometimes burdensome for students.

This is a challenge that often feels out of our control, subject to the preferences of private companies and legislators. Our job is to stay informed on the latest rules, and up to date on the latest technologies, such that we can make smart decisions about where and how to invest our resources. In addition, those of us who work in theological education can amplify conversations about open access and authors' rights, making sure that our faculty and colleagues continue to raise concerns about digital access with their publishers.

Second, given that our seminary population is comprised of a wide mix of students, diverse in age, background and technological skill, not all students are comfortable accessing digital materials. This intensifies the need for faculty and staff to right away train students to use reputable and scholarly resources, rather than simply jumping to AI and Google. In other words, how can we better [and earlier] encourage our students to swim in the deep end, rather than just splashing around in the shallows?

I am not confident that we are doing enough to realize Raber's vision of providing "scaffolded instruction for students around research and use of resources. Information and research needs vary at different points of study, and it would be helpful to have research skills mapped to courses in which the skills can be taught and practiced." As we all know, all students have increasing demands on their time, which means that sometimes students are not able to give serious attention to library research tools [and now I am speaking of both physical and digital tools] until their hour of need, which, as we know, might be 10 pm the night before a paper is due, and that is not the moment when nuanced learning can occur! We must work to develop more "point-of-need" tutorials (e.g., easily accessible video tutorials) that students can access on their own timelines. Faculty can encourage this engagement earlier, rather than later, in a student's seminary career, and in a specific seminary course.

Third, there continues to be a place for a physical library—not just for nostalgia, but for the ongoing mission of a theological institution. Wartburg Seminary's physical library is a welcoming "third space" of rest, study, and collaborative work. For our on-campus students who do not always have a quiet, distraction-free place to study at home, the library is a welcome place to come where the environment fosters deep thinking and creativity. Additionally, twice a year, our full student population is on campus for Prolog Week, a critical time of community building and education that is foundational for how we form our students. During these times, the library provides much-needed opportunities to access the physical library collection, receive hands-on research assistance, and huddle up to work on group projects—or just relax together and strengthen friendships.

Additionally, Wartburg is currently developing plans for an exhibit and meditation space on the second floor, which will invite community members to reflect critically on our past for the sake of the future, in order to continue to live into our identity as the kind of institution we want to be, and the kind of leaders we want to form: leaders the church and world so desperately needs. We believe that our investment in a brick and mortar library has a key role to play in this mission.

Finally, there is also an important archival role for the library (both digital and hard-copies) where historical materials, rare books and local historical documents find a home. Access to these resources is valuable for both seminary constituencies and outside patrons.

Wartburg Seminary is grateful to be a member of the Digital Theological Library, as it has greatly enhanced the resources we are able to offer to our distance learning students, and the quality of education we are able to offer them. At the same time, we continue to value the physical space of the library as the heart of an educational institution. In Wartburg's mission statement, we name ourselves as "a worship-centered community of critical theological reflection where learning leads to mission and mission informs learning." Reu Memorial Library, in its physical and digital forms, enables us to continue to live boldly into that mission—and will enable to do so into the future.

The Rev. Dr. Kristin Johnston Largen is the 15th president of Wartburg Theological Seminary, Dubuque, Iowa. She is an ordained minister in the Evangelical Lutheran Church of America, with a Ph.D. in Comparative Theology from the Graduate Theological Union, Berkeley, California. She is the author of many books, articles and book chapters. Her most recent book is *A Christian Exploration of Women's Bodies and Rebirth in Shin Buddhism* (Lexington Books, 2020).

Wartburg Theological Seminary serves Christ's church through the Evangelical Lutheran Church in America by being a worship-centered community of critical theological reflection where learning leads to mission and mission informs learning. In partnership with the local and global church Wartburg Seminary forms, equips and sends Christ-centered, resilient, and adaptive leaders who interpret, proclaim and live the gospel of Jesus Christ for the thriving of congregations and the healing of the world. Wartburg graduates are called to be leaders with a passion for Christ and compassion for communities. They will faithfully embody the story of Jesus Christ and invite others into this transformative story with hope and joy.

We Must Preserve Books at All Costs

Stanley E. Porter

The DTL project is invaluable not just for theological education but for western culture and its intellectual survival. This may seem like an extreme statement, and it is, intentionally so. But the preservation and even thriving of western culture is more than just a passing fancy or another current trend. Western culture is the mainstay of our civilization and, indeed, of theological education. That is where DTL has such a vital role to play.

In case some have not noticed, we live in an increasingly ephemeral, temporary, scientific environment (I hesitate to use the term culture), in which the latest fads, especially if they are wrapped in appropriate technology and make outrageous claims for themselves, seem to have greatest currency. We have lost sight of the fact that all these expressions of current life, whether good or (unfortunately) bad, are based upon the accumulation of human knowledge, and that means book culture—although I would argue that the negative expressions of it are truncated expressions or even misunderstandings of it.

Book culture cannot be underestimated. It provides the continuous line of connection from where we now are back to the foundations of our culture and society. There have been many wrong turns and misdeeds along the way, and I dare say that we are at one of those points in our environmental development even as I write, but it is because we finally remember—almost inevitably through reading—that there are other ways of thinking about things, other ways of doing things, and, most importantly, essential human and spiritual values that we must not just remember but practice if we will survive our current dilemma.

The Bible and theological studies of course play a central role in all of this because they provide the scriptural, theological, and ethical basis of the content of our western thought and development. In that regard, it is not just books that we are talking about. We are talking about access to books, and with them their writings and thereby their content, that puts us into an appropriate perspective in relation to what has come before us and, as much as we may try to avoid it, what will come about in the times ahead.

As a result, DTL serves an invaluable role in contemporary education and more. It is a fundamental element in the preservation and dissemination of knowledge that moves beyond simplistic answers to human problems to the fundamental ideas that have been thought, developed, and disseminated over the centuries, and it therefore lays the foundation for optimism that the human predicament is not as dire as it may seem, since we have been here before, if we had taken the time to read and find out about our past. However, we must remember through accessing these vital writings that we have choices and alternatives, and we must take them at appropriate times and for appropriate purposes.

Of course, DTL uses digital technology. It must, because the world in which we live utilizes digital knowledge. But the content of DTL is not just bits and bytes and the like. It is made up of books and similar materials, generated by millions of people over centuries and preserved so that we don't have to be victims of our present circumstances, without a guide to what has come before or will occur after. It is the preservation in accessible form of the record of our past and the prospect of our future—made accessible not just to the few but potentially to everyone who has a desire not to be simply a creature of the present but a fully human being in the present—that is, a person who knows, appreciates, critically reflects upon with others, and then deliberately and ethically acts upon that knowledge, even if taking a minority position, because they are a truly educated person, one who has read the great thoughts of the past and gained inspiration for the present and the future.

And we thought that DTL was simply a way to avoid having to buy so many books and to get quick access to lots of publications!

Stanley E. Porter, PhD, is President, Dean, and Professor of New Testament, and holder of the Roy A. Hope Chair in Christian Worldview at McMaster Divinity College, Hamilton, Ontario. He has degrees in English, New Testament, and linguistics. He has taught in all these subjects. Porter is the author or co-author of 38 volumes and the editor of over 105 others. His major area of specialization is Greek language and linguistics, where he has innovated various theories and methods regarding the Greek language. He has also published widely on most topics in New Testament studies, such as Paul, the Gospels, the Johannine literature, Acts, hermeneutics, the canon, biblical interpretation, the Septuagint, papyrology and epigraphy, and textual criticism.

McMaster Divinity College (MDC) is a theological seminary that traces its roots to the Toronto Baptist College of the late 19th century. An independent academic institution with its own board and senate, MDC caters to the broader evangelical church, with over forty different denominations among its students. MDC is accredited by the Association of Theological Schools in the U.S. and Canada, and continues to draw faculty and students engaged in both academic and ministry vocations.

MDC offers a range of degree programs tailored to both ministerial and academic paths. Among them are the Master of Divinity (MDiv), the Doctor of Practical Theology (DPT), and multiple Master of Arts tracks. McMaster also has PhD programs in biblical, theological, and ministry studies. Its academic structure distinguishes between "professional" and "research" streams and offers flexible course delivery modes (in-person, livestream, asynchronous online) to accommodate students in active ministry or those balancing other commitments.

Embracing Open Access Publishing in Biblical, Theological, and Religious Studies

Drew Baker

Over the past two decades, the landscape of academic publishing has been transformed by the rise of Open Access (OA) scholarship. Emerging first within the natural sciences and medicine, OA has gradually spread into the humanities and social sciences, reshaping how knowledge is produced, disseminated, and consumed. At its most basic, OA refers to the free, online availability of scholarly work, unencumbered by paywalls or restrictive licensing, and often with permissions for reuse that go beyond simply reading. For Biblical, theological, and religious studies, the implications of this shift are profound. Seminaries, whose mission is both academic and ecclesial, stand at the crossroads of this change. They not only produce scholarship but also steward it on behalf of faith communities and the wider world. This chapter argues that seminaries should embrace OA publishing as a moral, pedagogical, and missional imperative, aligning the distribution of scholarship with the values and responsibilities of theological education.

What Is Open Access?
Open Access is often misunderstood, sometimes dismissed as an experimental publishing fad or confused with questionable practices such as "predatory" journals. In fact, OA represents a robust and principled movement that began with the Budapest Open Access Initiative (2002),

followed by the Berlin Declaration (2003), both of which articulated the vision of free and unrestricted access to peer-reviewed research literature. Today, OA is recognized in multiple forms: Gold OA, where articles are freely available at the point of publication, often funded by article processing charges (APCs); Green OA, where authors deposit versions of their work in institutional or subject repositories; and Diamond or Platinum OA, which makes scholarship available without fees for either authors or readers, typically sustained by institutional or consortial support.

Theological scholarship has historically lagged behind the sciences in adopting OA, due in part to the smaller scale of theological publishing, the financial precarity of many theological presses, and lingering skepticism about quality. Yet in practice, OA journals and monographs are subject to the same standards of peer review, editorial oversight, and scholarly rigor as their subscription-based counterparts. The core difference is not in quality but in accessibility. Global directories such as the Directory of Open Access Journals (DOAJ) and the Directory of Open Access Books (DOAB) testify to the scope and vitality of the OA movement. They serve as trusted registries of peer-reviewed publications, allowing scholars, students, and libraries to identify reliable OA resources with confidence. For theological disciplines, which increasingly seek to connect with global partners, these directories represent a vital means of discovery and dissemination.

The Case for OA in Theological and Religious Studies
Ethical Commitments

Theological education exists to serve faith communities and society, not only to advance academic discourse. Theological scholarship, therefore, carries a moral dimension: it is intended to edify, inform, and equip communities of faith around the world. In this light, restricting scholarship to those who can afford expensive journal subscriptions or monograph purchases undermines the very ethos of theological work. Open Access dismantles such barriers, embodying values deeply resonant with religious commitments to hospitality, justice, and the free sharing of faith. For scholars and institutions shaped by these commitments, OA becomes not merely a pragmatic option but an ethical responsibility.

Pedagogical Benefits

The educational benefits of OA for seminaries are equally significant. Many theological libraries, particularly in smaller institutions, cannot afford comprehensive journal and monograph subscriptions. Students in the majority world often have even more limited access, relying on outdated or incomplete resources. By contrast, OA ensures that high-quality research is available to all, irrespective of geography or institutional wealth. Faculty can integrate OA resources directly into syllabi, confident that students will have access without financial burden. Furthermore, OA enhances collaborative learning: students and scholars can engage the same body of scholarship across institutions, continents, and traditions.

Missional Dimensions

The missional aspect of OA publishing should not be overlooked. Seminaries exist not only for the sake of their own students but also for faith communities and the world. Scholarship in Biblical, theological, and religious studies, when made openly available, functions as public theology, reaching pastors, lay leaders, and engaged lay readers. This is particularly vital in contexts where formal theological education is scarce. By embracing OA, seminaries extend their influence beyond campus walls, making their scholarship a form of service and witness in the broader mission of faith communities. The work of the Open Library of the Humanities, which provides a sustainable model for humanities journals through library consortial funding, offers a particularly relevant example for theological institutions. By eliminating author fees and subscription barriers, it demonstrates how academic communities can collectively bear the cost of knowledge-sharing, aligning with the collaborative spirit of theological education.

Addressing Challenges and Concerns

Despite its promise, OA faces real challenges. The economics of OA remain complex. The Gold OA model often relies on article processing charges (APCs), which can be prohibitive for scholars in underfunded institutions. However, alternatives exist: some publishers adopt Diamond OA models sustained by institutional funding or library consortia; others encourage Green OA self-archiving in repositories. Creative solutions, such as collaborative publishing platforms among seminaries, are beginning to emerge. For instance, DTL Press (an initiative rooted in theological education) provides a model of Diamond OA publishing specifically for Biblical and theological scholarship. By leveraging institutional support rather than APCs, it makes quality theological research freely available to a global audience.

Concerns about quality, though frequently voiced, are largely unfounded. Peer review remains a cornerstone of reputable OA publishing, and leading OA journals and presses in theology (for example, Open Theology, or OA imprints from Brill and de Gruyter) have established credibility. The challenge is not scholarly rigor but perception: many faculty and administrators remain unfamiliar with the breadth and legitimacy of OA options. Directories such as DOAJ and DOAB play a crucial role in countering this perception by curating lists of vetted, high-quality OA publications.

Sustainability is also a key concern. Theological publishers, especially those with long histories of producing high-quality monographs, rightly worry about revenue streams in an OA environment. Yet hybrid models—combining OA offerings with traditional sales or offering institutional sponsorships—demonstrate that sustainability is possible. Indeed, by increasing visibility and readership, OA can enhance rather than diminish the long-term impact of theological publishing.

The Seminary as Advocate and Leader

If OA is to take root in Biblical, theological, and religious studies, seminaries must play a leading role. This leadership can take several forms. At the institutional level, seminaries can adopt policies that encourage or require faculty to deposit published work in institutional repositories. They can integrate OA awareness into faculty development programs and recognize OA contributions in promotion and tenure processes.

Libraries, often underappreciated in these conversations, are essential allies in advancing OA. Seminary libraries can curate repositories, partner with consortia, and educate students and faculty about OA resources. They can also provide the technical infrastructure needed for long-term digital preservation, ensuring that OA scholarship remains accessible for future generations.

Beyond policy and infrastructure, seminaries can foster a culture of openness. This involves framing OA as an extension of theological values, linking the free sharing of scholarship with the gifts of faith. It means encouraging faculty and students to see OA not as a burden but as a vocation: the calling to make their work available to those who most need it. In so doing, seminaries can set a precedent for the wider academy, modeling how institutions can align scholarly practices with core values. Initiatives such as the Open Library of the Humanities and DTL Press demonstrate that seminaries and their partners need not passively adopt OA practices but can actively shape them in ways consistent with their mission.

Conclusion

The transition to Open Access is not merely a technical or financial issue; it is a theological and institutional one. For seminaries, the embrace of OA represents fidelity to their mission: to serve faith communities, empower students, and contribute to the public good. By making scholarship accessible to all, regardless of economic or geographic barriers, OA embodies the very values that theological education seeks to cultivate—justice, generosity, service, and truth.

Seminaries stand at a pivotal moment. They can either remain on the margins of this global shift, clinging to outdated publishing models, or they can seize the opportunity to lead, demonstrating how scholarship can be both excellent and open. Embracing OA is, in the end, not simply about publishing; it is about reimagining the vocation of theological scholarship for a global and digital age. Directories such as DOAJ and DOAB, infrastructures like the Open Library of the Humanities, and theological initiatives such as DTL Press together show a viable path forward. They embody a future in which theological scholarship is not locked away but shared freely, for the flourishing of faith communities and the academy alike.

Drew Baker (Ph.D., MLS) is the Managing Director and Chief Operations Officer at the Digital Theological Library. He has written on a range of topics including postcolonial ethics, user-generated metadata, and religion in the United States. He is the co-founder of the Digital Theological Library. He is the co-founder of the Digital Theological Library.

The Digital Theological Library (www.thedtl.org) is a nonprofit corporation co-owned by more than 100 seminaries. Its mission is to help everyone to engage in self-critical reflection upon their own faith and in humble dialogue with those of other traditions. The DTL fulfills this mission through the curation of digital library resources for its member institutions, religious professionals and interested individuals. The DTL also fulfills this mission through publishing religious studies content.

On the Timeliness and Sensibleness of a Digital and Collaborative Library

Kyle Roberts

I recall my first in-depth awareness of a distance seminary course over 25 years ago. It was essentially a correspondence course: A set of cassette tapes (record lectures) and an accompanying packet of reading materials, including a syllabus and assignment instructions. There was no synchronous interaction, just correspondence between the individual student and the professor via snail mail. Students would purchase their textbooks through the seminary's bookstore and receive them through the mail. Other, more advanced models were in use then, too, including emerging learning management systems and communication modules for students. But back then, distance education, including library and book access, was clearly at the edge of a frontier.

Theological education has been undergoing transformation for decades. I began teaching part-time in a seminary while I was completing my doctorate. Distance learning was still in its relative infancy but was beginning to demonstrate that it met a need. That need was, at the time, a marginal exception for those who couldn't afford the time and resources required to uproot, put jobs on hold, and become a full-time student in a physical learning community. In the decades since, that exception has become the norm. While the overall number of students in ATS (Association of Theological Schools) seminaries across the nation has increased over the past 25 years, the demographics have shifted dramatically. Those students take fewer credits at a time than students in past decades. They take courses primarily online, whether interacting live through video or on their own time through a learning management system. And most of now, it seems, take those courses wherever they already live and work.

Largely gone or reduced are the days-long, on-campus learning experiences with primarily local students attending classes on campus. United Theological Seminary of the Twin Cities, where I teach on the faculty and serve as Dean, has a growing and vibrant student community. But that community is dispersed across the nation and even the globe. At last count, over 70% of United students live outside of the Twin Cities metroplex area. That trend shows no signs of abating. While we maintain a dedicated and energetic local community, our seminary community is largely connected through digital means. We rely on technology to communicate, to interact, to teach and learn, to share ideas, to form and to be formed. United's story is replicated over and over across the landscape of seminary education.

Sadly, for many of us bibliophiles, the role of the physical library in this new reality has changed. The traditional on-campus library, once a hub of student community learning and life, takes up a proportionally large amount of real estate, but with decreasing signs of activity and interaction. Traditional interlibrary loan systems serve an important purpose. But when distance students are the norm rather than the exception, physical ILL is tedious and inefficient.

United Seminary discovered the Digital Theological Library at an opportune moment. How can we make the most of our resources to serve our changing student demographic? How can we provide ready and immediate access to essential theological resources (books, articles, journals) to students in their own local learning contexts? The Digital Theological Library provides access to a tremendous wealth of resources for our students and faculty through clicks and keystrokes, from wherever they are.

    The digital system isn't perfect. It does require a shift in aesthetic expectations and sensibilities. Many of us who chose theological education are drawn to the physicality of texts. We want to flip through a book or a journal, cracking it open, scanning it quickly or digesting it slowly. We may flip to the index and back again to our placeholder or dog-eared page. Many of these aesthetic experiences are now history with the turn to the digital age of books and reading. But in this new era of theological education, more is gained than is lost: The sheer volume at our students' and faculty members' fingertips; search functions; the ease of "copy and paste" for storing information. These capabilities are all transforming the way we read, research, write, and think. These transformations call for theological reflection and critical examination. But resisting the steady flow of change in the way that information is accessed will only be to the detriment of our students, of their learning. Resistance will also be to the detriment of our institutions, which require nimble, adaptable, and efficient methods of reaching a changing demographic of students.

    The Digital Theological Library provides a ready-made way to join a community of theological learning institutions, sharing resources to build a library which none of our institutions could develop on our own. It is no secret that in an industry where theological differences and a scarcity of resources contribute to the tendency to retrench and silo, our libraries have served as the exception. Those tending our libraries care about knowledge and knowledge access and worry less about ideological commitments and theological dividing markers. The shared commitment to pool resources for the sake of knowledge access in a changing marketplace is both timely and sensible.

Dr. Kyle Roberts currently serves as Vice-President for Academic Affairs and Dean at United Theological Seminary of the Twin Cities, where he also holds the Schilling Chair in Public Theology and the Church & Economic Life. His academic formation includes a PhD in Biblical and Systematic Theology from Trinity Evangelical Divinity School, an MDiv from Midwestern Baptist Theological Seminary, and a BA in Philosophy and Literature from Wheaton College. Roberts's scholarship spans Kierkegaard and modern theology, Christian social ethics, and biblical interpretation—he is the author of *Emerging Prophet: Kierkegaard and the Postmodern People of God* and co-author of *Matthew: The Two Horizons Commentary*. At United, he teaches courses ranging from Public Theology and Christian Ethics to electives such as Evil, Death and Alienation, Historical Theology (modern period), and Capstone Seminar.

United Theological Seminary of the Twin Cities is a progressive, ecumenical seminary located in St. Paul, Minnesota, rooted in the liberal Protestant tradition and historically affiliated with the United Church of Christ. Established in 1962 through the merger of Mission House Seminary (Wisconsin) and Yankton School of Theology (South Dakota), United now functions as an independent and multi-denominational school. The seminary offers graduate degrees including the Master of Divinity, Master of Arts (e.g. Religion & Theology, Leadership), and Doctor of Ministry, and is known for its emphasis on social justice, the arts, interfaith dialogue, and theological innovation. Its mission is to prepare compassionate, creative leaders for faith communities and society, engaging theological education toward justice and transformation.

The Great Benefit of the Digital Theological Library to the Entirely Online Theological Institution

Randall J. Pannell

The New School of Biblical Theology (NSBT) is a visionary learning environment that prepares men and women for the ministry challenges of the first quarter of the 21st century, especially in view of the cultural diversities in both North America and the entire globe. As primarily a master's level institution, it is an entirely online institution with something of an innovative instructional format. Typical online NSBT students cannot transplant themselves to study in a traditional classroom. Their need is to stay where they are and to be able to complete their ministerial educational requirements are the periphery of their lives. An online curriculum is their only option.

Significant to the master's level of theological education is the availability of a theological library. Given the disparate locations of the NSBT student, a brick-and-mortar library building is not practical nor effective. As far as it concerns NSBT, we could not deliver of degrees without the Digital Theological Library (DTL).

NSBT could not even exist, not to mention flourish, without the existence of the Digital Theological Library. Not only is the DTL available to the NSBT students via the NSBT learning software, it is also very affordable to the individual institution as well as to its student body. Volumes are available in PDF format to allow the professors to select specific data within assignments without having students purchase entire books that may not be useful to the specific curriculum of the individual course. As an instructor, it is also possible to grab PDF sections of texts and load them into the individual course giving immediate access to significant data for specific assignments within the course.

My particular and primary doctoral discipline is Semitic Languages and Literature. The DTL also allows me to stay up to date on my research but also to have access to significant data without the need to purchase books just for a single reference or so.

I was also on the DTL Board in the past, which gave me great insight to its operational integrity, as well as the camaraderie of other theological educators and administrators.

Given all the above, from my perspective, the primary benefit for any institution, especially the online institutions and programs, is the availability of such a tremendous inventory of scholarly and ministerially related books and articles. The DTL allows so many associated institutions to reach more students locally and worldwide with so many primary resources.

My friend and colleague at NSBT, Dr. Dale Irvin, has shared with me a significant perspective regarding this online world of research and study. He added that over the past decade we have seen a steady increase in students in all theological programs, not just those that are offered online, moving entirely to online resources for their research. The number of theological schools that have now gone entirely online are multiplying. For example, in a hybrid mode like Chicago Theological Seminary and McCormick are deploying short residential units with most of the coursework being done online. This means that more and more students are doing most, if not all, of their research online.

Even campus-based programs with residential housing and a physical library building within walking distance, like Princeton Seminary, have seen students opting to go online to find resources for research. Unfortunately, these students often end up in unreliable web sites, so much so that many schools have had to introduce into their orientation to research a component on how to judge and engage online resources for critical theological academic purposes. NSBT's having access to the DTL helps orient our online "seeker" students to a reliable academic site, without fear of compromise.

NSBT has a part of its mission to offer ministerial training to those already in ministry and those called to ministry within the network of NSBT's founders and their associates. NSBT is a relatively new institution. We are currently in the process of gaining accreditations that will allow us to provide the theological and ministerial education to our students within the United States and within NSBT's networks of ministries outside North America.

Over the coming decades we are going to see much more in the way of theological education expanding across Africa, Asia, and Latin America. As my colleague Dr. Irvin observes, "the models of theological education that seek to closely replicate the material delivery system of existing knowledge that has characterized the Western academy for centuries, *the library*, are very expensive to replicate in contexts of rapid development. Too often traditional libraries are stocked with donated material texts that libraries in the West no longer want which take up an inordinate amount of local resources to maintain especially in hotter climates." There is a growing body of theological work being done in Africa, Asia, and Latin America that is not generally available in the US or Europe due to lack of knowledge of publishers, gaps in acquisition policies, and simple arrogance.

Fortunately, Global DTL has begun to address this wealth of knowledge, if still only in a rudimentary way. It allows one to search in Portuguese, Spanish, French, and Mandarin. We have not seen many texts added yet in these languages, but it does indicate where theological education is going globally. Several major theological schools with existing libraries have tried to make acquisitions from the wider global context a priority but have not been able to sustain the effort. This is an area where the DTL, with its greater flexibility, and hopefully with added resources covering other languages such as Mandarin, Korean, Portuguese, or even Yoruba, will be able to help accelerate the global shift.

The DTL is serving as an important bridge between the more traditional disciplines and ways of accessing knowledge for research, and the new environment of online communication, learning, research, and knowledge. As a scholar of Hebrew and the Old Testament I made the leap in my own personal journey decades ago into the ubiquitous world of online learning. At first, it was difficult to maintain the traditional structures of biblical studies and biblical scholarship, which are heavily "text" oriented, while embracing the new, emerging world of online learning and online theological education. The DTL does not just allow one to merely pass back and forth between these worlds; it facilitates the journey. I find that once one gets into DTL, they tend then to move easily to other online learning platforms.

My colleague, Dr. Irvin, says that his own personal experience here was that he was generally reluctant to build his own online library until he began through NSBT interacting with the DTL. He was introduced to online teaching and learning two decades ago, but he remained strongly committed to the physical book in his hand. Once he began to work with the DTL, he found it was a smooth transition from the paper volume to the computer screen. He found himself looking for digital copies of other texts that he regularly used. Within a year he had downloaded more than 500 books, journals, and articles. He has now given away almost all his theological library in hard volumes that were collected over 4 decades. He says he no longer needs traditional print copies. He says, "DTL has been a bridge for me in this regard."

We at NSBT consider the Digital Theological Library to be one of the great assets in assisting the online New School of Theology fulfill its mission within the context of Global Christianity in the 21st century!

Dr. Pannell has a Ph.D. from Southwestern Baptist Seminary in Old Testament Literature and Semitic Languages. He has been a teacher in the Old Testament, Hebrew, Aramaic and other Semitic languages, both in Latin America (primarily in Buenos Aires, Argentina), as well as in several institutions in the United States. Along with his teaching, he has served as the Chief Academic Officer in several institutions, including presently in the New School of Biblical Theology. His principal research interests have been in making the Scriptures, especially the Old Testament, more useful within the church and to enhance the leadership within the local church, especially among church planters. Having lived and taught in Latin America for several years, these interests extend presently to serving the Latin church in San Antonio, TX.

The **New School of Biblical Theology** (NSBT) is a visionary learning environment that prepares men and women for the ministry challenges of the first quarter of the 21st century, especially in view of the cultural diversities in both North America and the entire globe. More than ever, an overall understanding of the Bible, along with the effective capacity to interpret it, and to minister within the diverse cultures of contemporary cultures, is vital. NSBT's mission is to foster its graduates' growth in the Spirit while preparing them to answer Christ's call to ministry and mission in the world today. The heart of NSBT's vision is to respond to the overwhelming need of leaders who are biblically trained to influence culture by navigating the nexus of Christian faith and culture.

Connecting Institutional Transformation and Decision-Making
Becoming an Early Adopter of the Digital Theological Library

Charisse L. Gillett

I remember the library of my childhood with fondness and nostalgia. The Stoney Island Library on the south side of Chicago was a beacon of hope and transformation as I tried to access and understand the world around me and beyond. Books and magazines, along with the quiet and stillness of the place, made this library one of my favorite childhood haunts. I loved looking at the book titles, flipping through the magazines and simply sitting at the table reading. Looking through the card catalog for a title or browsing it before checking out a book was part of the experience. This neighborhood library remains true to its important mission of bringing learning, education and knowledge to the community. How the library functions and the resources and services available to the community have shifted with the times. It is a change that is reflected in the seminary community I serve as well.

My love of learning and the library of my childhood hold a particular kind of space in my head and heart. These memories are connected to my sense of community, family, intellect and hopes and dreams for myself and my community. The Bosworth Memorial Library of Lexington Theological Seminary held the same connective tissue for many graduates, Seminary faculty and staff and members of the Lexington community. The Bosworth Library expanded the Seminary's presence in the Lexington area and connected students to their call to serve God. The books, magazines, monographs, pictures, paintings and resources in the library represented holy ground. Amid a remarkable institutional transformation beginning in 2010, the Seminary and its leadership grappled with how to transform the library to meet the needs of students who would access its services remotely. The presenting issues for the Board of Trustees, faculty and Seminary leadership were current and future costs; stable access to online resources for all students, with special attention to those living in remote areas: honoring the legacy of those who had cared for the library; and the impact of relocating the Seminary on the ability of the students, faculty and library patrons to access its resources.

    The Lexington Theological Seminary of the past is rooted in its origin story to provide theological education to pastors and laity in emerging communities of the Stone-Campbell tradition. This tradition revolves around the saying, "No Creed But Christ; No Book But the Bible." In 2013, LTS was grappling with a declaration of financial exigency, two lawsuits by faculty alleging discrimination, a fractured institutional culture, the sale of the campus and adjacent properties, relocation of the campus and an exciting but untested competency-based curriculum. Into this basket of delight, the librarian had approached the Vice President of Academic Affairs and Dean with idea of acquiring library resources through the also untested Digital Theological Library (DTL). The question for the VPAA & Dean, Faculty and President was, amid tremendous change, could LTS manage and communicate the need and value of another untested idea? Would this new iteration of the library push the school further into spaces of innovation and transformation, and if so, what would be the likely outcome?

It is helpful to remember that pre-Covid, the adoption of an online platform as a substantive pedagogical model for theological education was met with skepticism, and a competency-based theological educational model was received with even less appreciation. In this pre-Covid context, online education and the DTL had few early adopters. Lexington Theological Seminary, in confronting change on multiple levels, was one of those early adopters.

Librarian Dolores Yilibuw was a persistent advocate for the DTL. She understood almost immediately that the online component of the new curriculum and the geographic diversity of the student community would alter library services and expand tenfold the ways in which students accessed online resources. As a non-residential institution, providing students, faculty, staff and patrons with viable and reliable options for resources was critical. Simply put, changes in the Seminary's educational delivery model required changes in how library services were delivered and accessed by students, faculty and library patrons. Five opportunities for connecting transformation and decision making emerged.

1. **Connecting** the request to join DTL required communicating the reality that the library, like other aspects of institutional life, was changing and very little could stop the changes heading our way. The DTL, like online theological education, was unknown at the time but, as we now know, both were in fact models for the future.
2. **Connecting** the decision to become an early adopter of DTL meant connecting the decision to the Seminary's history and origin story as an institutional forerunner. Founded in 1865, LTS was

the first graduate theological school in covenant with the Christian Church (Disciples of Christ); was one of the first to enroll women and hire women on the faculty; and was an early supporter and adopter of the principles of what is now the Association of Theological Schools Commission on Accrediting. In the modern era, the Seminary was one of the first institutions to adopt field education, move to online education and call a woman and African American as the chief executive officer. In other words, Lexington Theological Seminary leaders and decision makers were historically risk takers.

3. **Connecting** the decision to become an early adopter of the DTL meant understanding current collection practice and policies. This discussion highlighted the reality that the Seminary in 10 years would need new partners to access the technology necessary to meet the requirements of a theological community that suddenly had to access resources largely in an online population.

4. **Connecting** the decision to become an early adopter of the DTL meant taking a risk and moving forward without answering important questions. Many of the questions about budget, acquisition practices and the number of libraries that might join in the new library venture were unanswerable. The DTL was for the LTS community was yet another untested experiment for the Seminary's head librarian it was an idea whose time had come. It simply needed time to mature. To participate in this venture was a risk that only time could validate.

5. **Connecting** the decision to become an early adopter of the DTL meant linking the decisions to the mission of the Seminary to prepare faithful leaders

for God's mission in the world and our institutional hopes for Lexington Theological Seminary.

The Bosworth Memorial Library of today, much like the library of my youth, is a vibrant center of learning undergirded by the technology of the day. This technology connects the libraries to those who need it and enables access to resources for communities that expand beyond traditional borders. The geographically dispersed LTS community continues to be supported by a library that provides materials that spur deep theological reflection, conversations fueled by scholars and meaningful encounters between what is known about God and what we must learn in the classrooms.

Dr. Charisse L. Gillett became the 17th president of Lexington Theological Seminary in 2011. She has led the institution in a period of transformation in theological education, the seminary's organizational life and shifts in political and social culture. She is a member of the ATS Board of Directors and the Chair of the Board of Directors for the In Trust Center for Theological Schools and she is working on a series of essays on institutional transformation.

Lexington Theological Seminary (LTS), founded in 1865 in Lexington, Kentucky, is a graduate theological institution affiliated with the Christian Church (Disciples of Christ) that pursues an intentionally ecumenical identity. It is accredited by the Association of Theological Schools and offers several degree programs including the Master of Divinity (M.Div.), Master of Theological Studies (MTS), Master of Pastoral Studies (MPS), and Doctor of Ministry (D.Min.). Lexington Seminary emphasizes flexible, competency-based and congregation-centered education—especially via online, hybrid, and intensive formats—designed to integrate theological formation with real-world ministry contexts.

Empowering Global Seminaries
AI-Enhanced Open Access Publishing via DTL Press

Thomas E. Phillips

Introduction

Theological education depends on textbooks. They shape the classroom experience, guide students into new disciplines, and transmit the accumulated wisdom of scholarly traditions. Yet textbooks in theology and religion are often prohibitively expensive, leaving many students and seminaries with limited or outdated resources. High costs restrict access, while slow publishing cycles delay the availability of new knowledge.

The DTL Press, launched under the nonprofit umbrella of the Digital Theological Library (DTL), addresses this crisis directly. Its mission is clear: to create and distribute affordable, high-quality textbooks for theological education that are freely available to anyone in the world. By combining the ethos of Open Access publishing with the practical advantages of artificial intelligence, DTL Press is reshaping how theological resources are produced and shared. This chapter explores how DTL Press's model ensures that theological education is more widely available, more affordable, and ultimately better.

DTL Press as a Model for Open Access Publishing

Unlike commercial publishers, whose textbook prices often place them out of reach for students and seminaries, DTL Press operates as a nonprofit with a pedagogical mission. It is supported by a group of seminaries committed to providing resources for global theological education. Its publishing program emphasizes the development of textbooks—introductory, intermediate, and advanced—that can be used in classrooms worldwide.

All titles are published in digital Open Access formats, ensuring free downloads for students and teachers. For those who prefer physical copies, print-on-demand services provide them at minimal cost. By leveraging AI in translation, editing, and typesetting, DTL Press can produce these textbooks efficiently and at scale, while preserving the quality and rigor expected of academic scholarship.

Accessibility: Widening Global Reach

Textbooks are only useful if students can access them. Too often, theological education in the Global South or in underfunded seminaries in the North has been limited by the inability to purchase required texts. DTL Press breaks this cycle by ensuring that any student, anywhere, can access its textbooks without charge.

AI expands this accessibility through rapid translation into English, Spanish, French, Portuguese, Haitian Creole, and other languages, making it possible for the same textbook to be available to diverse student bodies across the globe. Imagine a seminary class in Nigeria and another in Brazil working with the same theology text, each in their own language, without the burden of prohibitive costs. This multilingual, barrier-free access exemplifies the mission of DTL Press.

Affordability: Reducing Costs for Students and Institutions

The affordability crisis in theological education is particularly acute when it comes to textbooks. A single required volume can cost students more than they can reasonably afford, and libraries often cannot sustain subscriptions or purchases for every course.

DTL Press directly addresses this challenge by ensuring that its textbooks are free in digital form and inexpensive in print form. Students can download core course texts without financial strain, and seminaries can plan curricula knowing that required readings are available to all. This not only levels the playing field for students from different economic backgrounds but also allows professors to assign high-quality works without worrying about cost barriers.

AI contributes by reducing production costs. Automated tools for layout, editing, and translation ensure that DTL Press can produce textbooks without the overhead expenses that inflate prices in traditional publishing. The result is a sustainable model where affordability and quality reinforce one another.

Enhancing Quality through Collaboration

Affordable does not mean inferior. DTL Press is committed to high-quality textbooks that meet the standards of academic scholarship and pedagogical usefulness. AI supports this process by handling tasks such as consistency checks, formatting, and multilingual adaptation, but the intellectual and theological work remains firmly in the hands of scholars.

The Press's collaborative model ensures that each textbook is developed under the guidance of experienced scholars and peer review. For example, the "Theological Essentials" series uses AI-assisted drafting to accelerate production but requires close oversight by theologians who shape, refine, and approve the content. This partnership allows for efficiency without any compromise of academic depth. Students thus receive textbooks that are not only affordable but also academically robust and pedagogically sound.

Speed and Responsiveness

Textbooks must also be timely. Courses evolve as new questions arise—whether in biblical interpretation, ethics, or theology—and students need access to resources that reflect contemporary debates. Traditional publishing cycles, often stretching over years, leave classrooms lagging behind.

With AI-assisted workflows, DTL Press can produce textbooks more quickly. Editing, typesetting, and translation can be completed in months rather than years, enabling seminaries to respond nimbly to emerging issues. Professors can assign textbooks that are both current and accessible, ensuring that students engage with the best scholarship in real time.

Scalability Across Traditions and Contexts

Textbooks should serve diverse audiences, not only students in North American or European contexts. DTL Press designs its textbooks with scalability in mind. Through multilingual publication and cultural adaptation, its works can be used in seminaries across traditions, denominations, and regions.

AI makes this scalability possible. A core textbook in New Testament studies, for example, can be quickly adapted into Spanish, Portuguese, or French, making it equally valuable in seminaries in Latin America, West Africa, or Europe. By scaling across traditions and contexts, DTL Press ensures that theological education is enriched by common resources while remaining sensitive to diverse needs.

Empowering Authors and Scholars Worldwide

The creation of textbooks should not be limited to a handful of scholars in well-resourced institutions. DTL Press empowers all scholars, regardless of their location—whether in developed or developing nations—to both read and publish. By offering editorial and technological support, the Press makes it possible for scholars from underrepresented regions to contribute textbooks that reflect their contexts and perspectives.

AI lowers barriers by assisting with translation and formatting, while the Open Access model ensures that these textbooks reach students everywhere. A systematic theology textbook authored by a Kenyan scholar or a pastoral theology text by a Brazilian theologian can now circulate globally, enriching classrooms with voices often excluded from traditional publishing pipelines.

Institutional Alignment and Mission

For seminaries, investing in textbook production through DTL Press is not merely a pragmatic choice; it is a direct expression of mission. Seminaries exist to form leaders for communities of faith and to provide students with the tools they need for ministry and scholarship. By producing textbooks that are both affordable and high quality, DTL Press strengthens this mission.

Because DTL Press is rooted in the nonprofit infrastructure of the Digital Theological Library and supported by a group of seminaries, it is aligned with the shared purpose of making theological education widely accessible. Its textbooks embody the seminary's dual commitment to academic rigor and service to global communities of faith.

Building Shared Infrastructure

The success of DTL Press rests on shared commitment. By pooling resources and expertise across a group of seminaries, the Digital Theological Library has already expanded access to scholarly resources. DTL Press extends this vision by creating a shared publishing platform for textbooks.

This collaborative infrastructure reduces costs for individual institutions while multiplying benefits for all. It shows that when seminaries work together, they can produce textbooks that are affordable, excellent, and globally available—something no single institution could easily achieve on its own.

Future-Oriented Theological Education

Textbooks are foundational to theological education, and the future demands that they be affordable, accessible, and adaptable. DTL Press's AI-enhanced Open Access model positions seminaries to meet this demand. Students today—and the pastors, chaplains, and scholars they will become—need to learn in a world where digital resources are abundant but unevenly distributed.

By modeling a future-oriented approach to textbook publishing, DTL Press demonstrates that seminaries can both preserve the integrity of theological scholarship and embrace innovative methods. The result is theological education that is not only current but also equitable, global, and mission-driven.

Conclusion

The integration of Open Access publishing with AI workflows, as embodied by DTL Press, represents a breakthrough in the creation of theological textbooks. By producing affordable, high-quality textbooks that are accessible to students everywhere, DTL Press addresses one of the most pressing needs of theological education. It widens access, reduces costs, ensures academic quality, empowers global scholars, and strengthens seminary missions.

For seminary administrators, the message is clear: supporting initiatives like DTL Press is not simply a matter of adopting new technology, but of fulfilling the mission of theological education itself. By embracing AI-enhanced Open Access publishing, we extend the reach of our classrooms, equip students without burdening them financially, and ensure that theological education remains a gift available to all.

Note: This article was created by AI in less than 30 minutes of prompt enginneering. For more on the use of AI in theological education, see Thomas E. Phillips, *AI and Theological Education* (El Cajon: DTL Press, 2025) and Heather Shellabarger, *AI and Theological Pedagogy: A Bloom's Taxonomy Approach for Graduate Seminaries* (El Cajon: DTL Press, 2025).

The DTL Press is the publisher of this and many other Open Access titles in several different languages. *www.DTLPress.org.*

Afterward

As we bring this collection to a close, we are grateful for the voices represented here. Each essay reflects a willingness to wrestle with the tension between what has been and what could be. Authors have drawn from traditions that ground us, named the challenges that confront us, and offered experiments that push us to imagine alternative futures.

As editors, we appreciated the openness to possibility that runs throughout these reflections. Again and again, the essays remind us that theological education is not fixed but always in motion, shaped by the people and communities who practice it. The variety of perspectives collected here underscores that there is no single way forward, but there is a shared desire to serve faithfully in a time of disruption and change.

In our interactions with contributors, we also found the conversations circling around something that rarely appeared directly in the essays. Behind the written reflections lay a deeper struggle with the assumptions that shape theological education itself. Authors often spoke about the weight of expectations carried by accrediting bodies, denominational traditions, and institutional histories. Those assumptions about what learning is and how it should take place continue to frame the way we imagine both present practices and future possibilities. Even when pursuing innovation, it is easy to carry forward the very frameworks we hope to reimagine. Greg Henson has referred to this dynamic as Organizational Formation, a way of naming how organizations themselves are continually shaped by the assumptions and practices they embody. Future conversations need to press further into these realities, moving beyond adjustments to methods and models toward a deeper examination of the assumptions that quietly guide them.

Our hope is that readers carry these reflections as invitations to continue the conversation. The essays here open important doors, but there is still more work to be done. We look forward to seeing how others will take up these questions, test them in practice, and push even deeper into the possibilities for theological education.

GH
TEP

Bibliography

Bessel van der Kolk, *The Body Keeps the Score*. London: Penguin, 2014.

Cannell, Linda M. "Theology, Spiritual Formation and Theological Education: Reflections Toward Application." *Life in the Spirit: Spiritual Formation in Theological Perspective.* Edited by Jeffrey P. Greenman and George Kalantzis. Downers Grove, IL: InterVarsity Press, 2010.

_____. *Theological Education Matters: Leadership Education for the Church.* Newburgh, IN: EDCOT Press, 2006.

Gans, Joshua. *The Disruption Dilemma*. Cambridge: MIT Press, 2017.

Glanzer, Perry L. "Are You Trying to Create Experts or Mentor Students toward Excellence? The Two Are Not the Same." *Christian Scholar's Review* (blog), September 3, 2025. https://web.archive.org/save/https://christianscholars.com/are-you-trying-to-create-experts-or-mentor-students-toward-excellence-this-fall-the-two-are-not-the-same/

Gonzalez, Justo L. *The History of Theological Education.* Nashville: Abingdon, 2015.

Kalsched, Donald. "Revisioning Fordham's 'Defences of the Self' in Light of Modern Relational Theory and Contemporary Neuroscience." *The Journal of Analytical Psychology* 60.4 (2015): 477-80.

Keller, Catherine. *Face of the Deep: A Theology of Becoming.* New York and London: Routledge, 2003.

Miller, Lisa. *The Awakened Brain*. Dublin: Allen Lane, 2021.

Phillips, Thomas E. *AI and Theological Education* (El Cajon: DTL Press, 2025)

Pui-lan, Kwok. *Postcolonial Imagination and Feminist Theology.* Louisville: Westminster John Knox Press, 2005.

Severan, A. *Metamodernism and the Return of Transcendence.* Amazon CreateSpace: 2021.

Shaw, Perry. *Transforming Theological Education: A Practical Handbook for Integrative Learning.* 2nd ed.; Carlisle, Cumbria: Langham Publishing, 2022.

Shellabarger, Heather. *AI and Theological Pedagogy: A Bloom's Taxonomy Approach for Graduate Seminaries* (El Cajon: DTL Press, 2025).

Smith, Ted A. *The End of Theological Education.* Grand Rapids: Eerdmans, 2023.

Sun, Chloe T. *Attempt Great Things for God: Theological Education in Diaspora.* Grand Rapids: William B. Eerdmans Publishing Company, 2020.

Sweet, Leonard. *Rings of Fire: Walking in Faith through a Volcanic Future.* Colorado Springs: NavPress, 2019.

Vermeulen, Timotheus and Robin van den Akker. "Notes on Metamodernism." *Journal of Aesthetics and Culture* 2.1 (2010): 56-77.

Westhelle, Vitor. *Eschatology and Space: The Lost Dimension in Theology Past and Present.* New York: Palgrave Macmillan, 2012.

www.ingramcontent.com/pod-product-compliance
Lightning Source LLC
Chambersburg PA
CBHW070647160426
43194CB00009B/1619